LICENSE TO PAWN

DEALS, STEALS, AND MY LIFE AT THE GOLD & SILVER

RICK HARRISON

WITH TIM KEOWN

HYPERION
NEW YORK

Library of Congress Cataloging-in-Publication Data

Harrison, Rick.
  License to pawn : deals, steals, and my life at the Gold & Silver / by Rick Harrison with Tim Keown. — 1st ed.
     p. cm.
   ISBN 978-1-4013-2430-8 (hardback)
  1. Harrison, Rick. 2. Pawnbrokers—Nevada—Las Vegas. 3. World Famous Gold and Silver Pawn Shop (Las Vegas, Nev.) 4. Fathers and sons—Nevada—Las Vegas. I. Keown, Tim. II. Title.
  HG2103.L37H37 2011
  332.3'4092—dc22
  [B]
     2010051138

Design by Renato Stanisic

FIRST EDITION

10   9   8   7   6   5   4   3   2   1

SUSTAINABLE FORESTRY INITIATIVE — Certified Fiber Sourcing — www.sfiprogram.org

THIS LABEL APPLIES TO TEXT STOCK

We try to produce the most beautiful books possible, and we are also extremely concerned about the impact of our manufacturing process on the forests of the world and the environment as a whole. Accordingly, we've made sure that all of the paper we use has been certified as coming from forests that are managed, to ensure the protection of the people and wildlife dependent upon them.

TO MY FATHER, "THE OLD MAN"

CONTENTS

CONTENTS

INTRODUCTION

his is my story, my family's story, and the story of the World Famous Gold & Silver Pawn Shop. It's also the story of Las Vegas, or at least a small slice of it, and the story of a world of characters unlike any you've ever encountered. One thing about my life: It's never boring.

After twenty-two years in the family-run pawn business, all of them with my dad and most of them with my son, I've seen just about everything. But the minute I think I've seen *everything*, that nothing left in this world possesses the capacity to surprise me, I'm confronted with something else that makes me shake my head in utter disbelief. It's seriously the greatest life I could imagine living.

I've dealt with every kind of human imaginable—billionaires and pimps, celebrities and crack whores, prim little old ladies and two-toothed meth addicts. I've had a conversation with Bill Clinton in a room with just ten other people, and I've battled to the death with some two-bit local politicians who think they're running the entire world.

I've learned a lot for being a tenth-grade dropout. Along the way, I've had a hell of a lot of fun. I've seen exultation and despair. I've been sweet-talked by beautiful women and cursed by tweakers who walk up to our infamous night window trying to convince me to give them $1,000 for their PlayStation games.

This is a big, crazy world, and most of the time I feel like I'm at the epicenter. Endlessly fascinating. It's impossible to be bored, impossible to be disengaged.

When I was a kid growing up in San Diego, I always loved to sit along the boardwalk in Mission Beach and just watch the people. I could amuse myself for hours that way. That's another beautiful thing about my job: Now I get to people-watch for a living.

This is the greatest business in the world. Every day is different, every person is different. I've always been a spastic, talky guy, and even before *Pawn Stars* came along and turned our shop into a kaleidoscope of people and cameras, I still would sit around and talk to people all day long. I can argue any side of any issue. I can talk politics forever, and I'll drive you crazy because I can argue against Republicans and Democrats equally. I've always got a better idea.

I don't judge anybody. There's room for everybody. My background gives me a unique perspective on people; as you will soon learn, my childhood was one long experiment in proving that smart people can do stupid things. I can relate to just about everybody, including people who are down on their luck and trying to scrape enough money together to get back into the casino to make that next big score. (They always think it's coming, trust me.)

I'll always remember a grumpy old lady who wandered through the shop several years ago wearing a judgmental look on her face. This grizzled old gal apparently expected something different from Gold & Silver Pawn, and she expressed her disgust by asking me, "You call this place 'World Famous Gold & Silver Pawn Shop.' Tell me: Why is this place 'World Famous'?"

I laughed a little, shrugged, and said, "Why? Because we put it on the sign, that's why."

I can't claim that Old Man and I had a premonition when we decided to include those two words on the sign. It was probably more wishful thinking than anything else, but twenty-two years later we can lay a claim to being *world famous*. We have *Pawn Stars* to thank for that. Our reality show is now shown on History in Australia and Canada, so if that little old lady ever comes back, I'll have a better answer for her.

If my life is a book—and I guess what you're reading proves it is—then Las Vegas is a major character in the saga. The place, the people, the politics—all of it weaves together to create a wild tapestry that is often hard to believe.

This is my journey. It hasn't always been easy, but it's always been fun. Enjoy the ride. Along the way, you'll hear from my son, Corey, known better as "Big Hoss" because of his size and big personality. And you'll hear from my dad, known better as "Old Man" because he's an old man. (True story: He got the nickname when he was in his thirties, because he's always been an old soul.) You'll also hear from Austin Russell, the world's most unlikely television star, known as "Chumlee" because he looks like a cartoon walrus.

If you don't know how a pawn shop works—and many people in "reputable society" don't—here's a primer:

The majority of our business, probably 60 percent, consists of pawns. If someone sells an item, it's straightforward. They get their money, always in cash, and I get the item. If an item is pawned, it's a loan. We charge a five-dollar device fee and 10 percent interest per month.

On *Pawn Stars*, the vast majority of the customers you see are selling, not pawning. There's a simple reason for that: Most people who are in the position where they have to pawn something don't want to be shown on television. There's a stigma attached to it, which is why it's legally considered a private transaction between the pawnbroker and the customer.

When you pawn an item, you have three options: (1) You can pay the interest each month—say, fifty bucks on a $500 loan—and I'll keep your stuff indefinitely; (2) you can pick your stuff up by paying the loan and the accrued interest; or (3) you can walk away and never come back, which means you don't owe me a dime, but your item becomes mine after 120 days and can legally be sold in the shop.

Every transaction, pawn or sale, is downloaded to both the Las Vegas Metro Police Department and Homeland Security. (That's a little-known aspect of the Patriot Act.) By law, any item I purchase or take on pawn must sit in the shop for a thirty-day waiting period while it is cleared by the police as not stolen.

There's nothing predictable about life in the World Famous Gold & Silver Pawn Shop. Old Man might be grumpy and Chumlee might do something stupid, but the swirl of crazy people and crazy stuff is unending. As I say on the open to the show, "You never know what's going to *come* through that door." All you have to do is spend a little time inside to see how true that statement is.

I'm Rick Harrison, and *this* is my pawn shop.

THE STORM IN MY HEAD

I WAS EIGHT YEARS OLD, LYING ON MY BED, when the world turned upside down. All of a sudden, no warning, without me moving, the floor became the ceiling and the ceiling became the floor. My head buzzed and crackled like a thousand power lines, and the world tilted on its axis. Slowly at first, then faster, until I was no longer aware of any of it.

I awoke later. I don't know how much later. I didn't know what had happened. My tongue felt like hamburger and my body felt as if it had been beaten with hammers. My legs were stiff and painful, my back hurt and my head held the residual buzz of whatever Category 5 electrical storm had struck it.

My parents' room was downstairs. My only thought was to get there; they would know how to handle this. My legs were cramped and constricted. I tasted blood from my shredded tongue. I was scared and confused and tired and just so goddamned scared. I got to my parents' room and knew from the looks on their faces that everything would be different from this point forward.

My first grand mal epileptic seizure, and the countless ones that followed, would define my childhood and much of my life. They struck violently and without warning. They struck mostly at night, and thankfully never at school. They struck with such severe force that I accepted it as a given that I would not live into adulthood.

Surely, at some point, one of these vengeful, raging attacks would cross the line. It would hit with all its wild, paralyzing fury, and I would simply never regain consciousness. From the time the seizures became a regular part of my life, I resigned myself to the idea that they would eventually kill me.

They altered my life in nearly every way. Whenever one hit, I would be out of school for as long as ten days. The muscle pulls were so painful and severe that I could do nothing but lay in bed with ice packs on my hamstrings and quadriceps.

It was there, in that bed in our suburban home in the Mission Valley section of San Diego, that my life changed again. I couldn't do anything. I couldn't move more than a few inches without pain. I didn't have a television in my room. Video games and iPads hadn't been invented. I was left to my own devices.

So I read books.

A lot of books.

I fell in love with a series of books called *The Great Brain*. These were the first books that captured my imagination. Written by John D. Fitzgerald, about a ten-year-old boy named Tom D. Fitzgerald, narrated by a younger brother known as J.D., *The Great Brain* allowed me to escape into a different world, a world I couldn't have. I would lose myself inside the pages.

The hero—owner of The Great Brain in question—lived in Utah and had these wonderful adventures that always centered on his ability to conjure a scheme that would make him money. He was a generous schemer, a con artist with a big heart. He'd do things like build a roller coaster in his backyard and charge to let people ride it, but there was always some twist at the end that caused him to have a crisis of conscience and give all the money back.

The Great Brain knew how to do everything: rescue friends who were trapped in a well; help a buddy deal with losing a leg; build that roller coaster. His world was my escape, my entree into a world outside the confines of my bedroom's four walls. I couldn't walk. I couldn't go to school. All I had were my ice packs and my books, so I made the best of it.

I have a very analytical, mathematical, calculating mind. I know I'm not supposed to believe in things like karma. But certain things have happened in my life that can't be explained by simple coincidence. How else can you explain the sequence of events and circumstances that led to me turning those bedridden hours—which should have been the worst hours of my life—into something that would provide a foundation for a life of curiosity and fun?

That's what happened. That's how profound the discovery of books was in my life. I didn't like school, but I loved books. Reading has been the basis of just about everything that came after. In that bed, I fell in love not only with books but with knowledge. The experience tapped into something I might never have found without the trying circumstances that led up to it. So much of the enjoyment I've gained from life has stemmed from a book—either researching some arcane item or reading to learn how to do something practical with my hands.

And how about the books I chose to read? Can it be explained away as mere coincidence that I chose a series of books about a kid my age who had an interest in making money and hustling to get it? I guess coincidence could explain it, and you're welcome to believe that. However, I have my doubts.

I WAS BORN IN North Carolina, where my parents were raised. Their courtship was unlikely, to say the least. My mom comes from a very proper, accomplished Southern family. Her father was a county judge and eventually became one of the lead attorneys for Philip Morris in North

Carolina. I have two cousins on my mom's side who work for Jet Propulsion Lab. My uncle was one of the lead designers on the space station and does satellite delivery systems. My cousins developed one of the first wireless Internet systems, which they sold for stock in an Internet company, unfortunately for them.

And my dad's side? Well, you might not be surprised to learn his family was a little less refined. They were dirt-poor white trash, left to survive on their wits for the most part. My dad was always a hustler, that's for sure. Old Man drove the school bus when he was fourteen. It apparently was legal to do that in North Carolina back in the 1950s. That was the law: You had to be at least fourteen years old to drive the school bus. Can you imagine an *eighteen*-year-old being allowed to do that now? Old Man got paid for it, of course—five or six dollars a week. He parked the bus at his house every night; he got up in the morning, picked up all the kids, and then parked the bus at the school during the school hours. When school got out, he would drop the kids off and park the bus at home.

But he wasn't always a pillar of responsibility. When he was seventeen, my dad stole a car, and he got caught. He appeared before the judge, and the judge said, "Son, do you want to go to jail or the military?" I assume my dad, pragmatic guy that he is, didn't waste a lot of time pondering this one. He chose the military.

My parents met at a barn dance when they were seventeen, before my dad left to join the navy. How's that for Americana? My mom was dragged to this dance by her friends—she had no interest in going—and when she saw my dad, she was attracted to him because he was really, really tan from working construction jobs. She thought he was Latin, if you can believe that. If she'd known he was a backwoods hick, she might have never spoken to him.

* * * *

I WAS BORN IN 1965, and we moved to San Diego when I was two, after my dad was transferred by the navy. There was hardship in my family before I was diagnosed with epilepsy, which might have something to do with how I handled it. The Harrisons were stoic, not big on feeling sorry for ourselves. There was some history behind that, too.

My parents were eighteen when they married, and because this was the 1950s, she got pregnant almost immediately. They had a daughter, my sister Sherry, who was born with Down syndrome. My dad had been in the navy for three years around the time Sherry was born, and when her medical bills became too expensive for the family to keep up, he re-enlisted for the health care benefits. Sherry died at six years old, when I was two, so I never really knew her.

We lived in the Mission Valley area, not far from Jack Murphy Stadium. If you take away the unfortunate grand mal epileptic seizures, it was a comfortable, happy childhood. People are surprised when I tell them I wasn't taunted or teased for my epilepsy, but I wasn't. My brother Joe was a typically vicious older brother, so I knew how to fight, but mostly my friends were just my friends. They accepted me for what I was, and they really didn't look at me any differently. I missed chunks of school in the wake of my seizures, but when I came back we took up where we left off. I don't have any indelible scars. At least I don't think I do. Others might disagree.

San Diego is the ultimate navy town, and when we moved there in 1967 it was beginning to boom. It was a different world for my parents—faster pace, more opportunity—and my mom took advantage by getting her real estate license and opening an office in 1970. You couldn't help but make money in real estate in San Diego around that time.

As you might expect from a future pawnbroker, my dad also ran various businesses on the side. He bought and sold gold, and he helped my mom with the real estate business. One of my fondest memories is going around on Saturday mornings with my dad and working on old, decrepit houses he and my mom picked up as rental units. We did everything our-selves, and some of these places probably should have been condemned.

Hustling was nothing new for the Old Man. Back in the day—my dad says "back in the day" for anything that happened before last week—he served as a paymaster on navy ships. As he tells it, it was nearly a physical impossibility for sailors to make their money last from one payday to the next. Every time the ship docked, they'd be out of money. So my dad figured he'd make this work to his advantage. He let it be known that he could provide loans to broke sailors. Remember, this was long before payday advance stores, and long before he had any idea he was going to be a famous Las Vegas pawnbroker and television star.

His deal was simple, and as old as money itself: He would give them an advance on their next check, lay out the terms of the interest, and then take his share—the interest, or vig—out of the next check. He made a good amount of side income on the deal, and there were times when he had to take a truck down to the pier to bring home the stuff he acquired on his trips through exotic spots like Southeast Asia and Europe.

He brought home toys for us kids, jewelry for my mom. We had a sweet Sony stereo before anyone I knew. Old Man was a pawnbroker before he was a pawnbroker.

There were nights on the ship when Old Man would tell everyone he was having a blackjack game in his room. Because the men were bored to tears living on a ship, he'd never have trouble filling out a game. Well, it turns out he wasn't really playing blackjack; he was the dealer. He was dealing the cards and making all kinds of money and nobody thought much of it. Sometimes sailors would lose big and start complaining about the cash, and he'd ask them what else they might have to pay him with. One time a guy said, "I just bought my wife a new set of china in Hong Kong."

Well, when my dad got home, my mom had a new set of china.

* * * *

MY MOM WAS A woman of her time. As the feminist movement caught hold in the 1970s, she ran with it. The 1950s archetype of the housewife with dinner on the table and a smile on her face had pretty much run its course, and my mom was not having any of it.

There was a television commercial around that time for a perfume called Enjoli. Its jingle, a reimagining of the Peggy Lee song "I'm a Woman," was famous at the time. It depicted a woman of the moment, bringing home the bacon, frying it up in a pan, and still somehow retaining her feminine side.

It was a new era, and my mom was a new-era woman. That message—that a woman could do it all and then some—was delivered into America's living rooms in a million different forms. It blasted through the television and right into my childhood. My mom was liberated.

With both parents working, the supervision wasn't what you'd call exceptional. They were off doing their own thing—which was fine—and we were, too. I had the kind of freedom that most of today's kids, with their helicopter parents and ultra-organized schedules, could never dream of having. Most of them wouldn't know what to do with it, either, from what I can tell. My friends and I would get into all kinds of trouble: going to Padres games and hopping the fence one after the other when the security guard wasn't looking (try doing that now); running free in the neighborhood climbing fences to eat the neighbors' oranges; shooting at each other with BB guns without regard to collateral damage.

It's worth repeating that my epilepsy had a major impact on my overall mind-set. With each successive seizure, I believed I was that much closer to death. This was just something I understood to be real, without much in the way of evidence, but those episodes were so goddamned frightening that I was left with no other conclusion.

So I reacted to it by really not giving much of a damn about anything. I was open to any adventure and any new experience, no matter how dangerous. I was still missing weeks of school at a time, and I was deathly bored when I was in school, and the medication I took didn't help. Back in the seventies, the only known treatment for epilepsy was barbiturates, in my case phenobarbital. This was the era of people running around with tongue depressors, trying to keep an epileptic from swallowing his tongue.

I have no idea what kind of damage those drugs did to my body over the years.

The drugs didn't seem to help stop the seizures. I averaged one every six weeks or so. I could feel them coming on but could do nothing to stop them. I'd be sitting in front of the television and it would be absolutely fucking terrifying: There would be this gathering storm in my head, the world would turn upside down, and then the world would shut off as quickly as if I'd flipped a switch in my brain.

For those few conscious seconds at the beginning of a seizure, every sense went into overdrive. It seemed as if all the circuits blew, and then my body would shut down.

They were terrifying and, in a weird way, liberating. They freed me up to do whatever the hell I wanted, and I became a terrible kid. Just awful. One of the worst. I have no problem admitting it, and there's no way to overstate it. I learned to live for the moment and enjoy the hell out of everything I did. That hasn't changed. I loved sports but couldn't play them because my mom lived in mortal fear that I would get hit on the head. While my brothers and friends were playing baseball, I couldn't. So, in a perverse twist, I became an adrenaline junkie. I loved anything that went fast and possessed an element of danger. And more than a few times, I smacked my head hard enough to give my mom a heart attack— had she only known.

Just like on *Pawn Stars*, in my everyday life I am prone to embarking on lengthy and barely relevant tangents when something either strikes me as interesting or bugs the crap out of me. Forgive me in advance, but here's one such instance:

I have a real fear of government-run health care. There's one reason: I lived it. If you don't know what it was like to navigate the rivers and tributaries of the military health-care system as an epileptic child of the 1970s, I'm about to change that.

My mom and I would show up at Balboa Hospital—the biggest hospital on the West Coast—at 7 A.M. We would park and get onto a tram like the ones they have at Disneyland and have it drop us off at Medical Records. We would wait there for an hour to get my records. Someone would go in the back and root around for an hour and then come out carrying a big box with all my records inside. We would take the box to the doctor's office.

Once at the doctor's office, we'd sit around and wait for probably another hour. There weren't real neurologists working for the navy at the time, or if there were they didn't stick around very long, so usually I would see a new doctor every four or five months. I'd finally get in to see the doctor, and he would sit there and review my records and then say, "OK, let's get some blood tests."

(Once I remember having to go back two weeks in a row because someone in the lab lost the fluid they extracted during a spinal tap. Two spinal taps in one week—now *that's* a good time.)

So my mom and I would scoop up the records and go to the lab and have them take my blood for the tests. By now it would be lunchtime, and so everything closed up and we'd go get some lunch. When lunch was over, we'd head back to the doctor's office to see if the blood work had come back yet. They were checking to see if my medication levels were OK, and most of the time the doctor wanted to tweak the prescription some, so he'd say, "Here's your prescription—head over to the pharmacy and get it filled."

So my mom and I would trudge over to the pharmacy and stand in line with what seemed like hundreds of old retired navy people. We'd drop off the prescription and be told our wait was an hour.

We'd kill that hour by going and getting me a haircut on the grounds or heading into the commissary for a few things my mom might need. Then we'd head back over to the pharmacy and pick up the prescription and head home.

This happened once a month, and it was an ordeal. We wouldn't get back on that tram to take us to our car until three or four o'clock in the afternoon.

When I think back on it, my mom had some saintly patience in those days. The time and effort it took to take care of a child with my health problems were significant. But there was one benefit to those monthly Doctor Days: It was the one day I knew I got to spend with my mom.

HERE'S HOW A TYPICAL school day went for me: I would take a pill in the morning before school, and by lunchtime it was a battle to the death to see if I could stay awake long enough to make it to lunch. Then, after lunch, it was usually a losing battle. I would almost always clunk my head on the desk and be out cold for much of the first period of the afternoon.

It wasn't long before phenobarbital wasn't the only drug I was ingesting. In fourth grade, I smoked pot for the first time. *Fourth grade.* Nine years old. We had a babysitter, and she apparently couldn't make it through a shift without smoking weed. She toked up right in our living room, and she must have noticed the way I was looking at her.

"Do you want to try some?" she asked.

"Sure," I said.

That ended up being my go-to answer.

"Do you want some (fill in the drug name here)?"

"Sure."

"Do you want to dive off that cliff?"

"Sure."

I was willing to do anything. I was *that* kid. Consequences never factored into the equation.

Take school, for example. I didn't think there was a good reason for me to keep going. The seizures made me miss an average of one week out of every six, so I always fell behind in my work and didn't really care about catching up.

Nobody ever asked to see my report card. Nobody asked what I did that day in school. My dad was a workaholic, my mom was a workaholic. If you get right down to it, they didn't pay enough attention to us. I don't hold it against them, but it's the truth. I'm sure they'd never admit it, but it's the truth. I gradually began to lose interest when I got to middle school.

My mind worked on principles of mathematical certainty. I know that sounds heavy, but even then I was calculating and analytical. Every time I had a seizure, I felt like I died a little. This feeling grew stronger as the years wore on, and by the time I was in eighth grade it had metastasized into an actual scenario: I was going to be walking down a flight of stairs, have a seizure, fall down, and die.

School wasn't the place I wanted to spend my days. The prolonged absences made it awkward, but more than that, I was one of those kids that just didn't fit. Teachers couldn't figure me out. I was a puzzle; I could go through complex math problems in my head with no problem, but I didn't fit the profile of the smart kid. I was a fuckup, and in our institutional educational system, fuckups don't get the benefit of the doubt.

School pretty much died for me when I was in eighth grade at Taft Middle School in San Diego. The first class after lunch was an advanced math class. Because of the epilepsy drugs, I'd fall asleep without fail, and the teacher was a complete ass. This was a bad combination for me.

Math was always easy for me; I knew from the time I was nine or ten that I kicked ass in math. Nothing they were teaching even remotely challenged me, but since I was labeled a bad kid—OK, since I *was* a bad kid—nobody ever took the time to acknowledge my intelligence.

This teacher hated me. The work we were doing was well below my skill level, even though it was supposedly an advanced class. I never did my homework, and yet at the end of the week we'd have a test on the material and I'd go through that thing—*bam-bam-bam*—in no time. I'd get every answer correct and never show my work. I could do everything in my head, and I didn't see the point of going through every step just to placate some teacher I didn't like in the first place.

So Mr. Asshole came to the only conclusion his little mind would allow: I was cheating.

I was falling asleep every day because of the phenobarbital, I wasn't paying attention, I wasn't doing my homework and I was getting 100 percent on every test without showing a stitch of work. Plus, Rick Harrison was a fuckup. Therefore, Rick Harrison must be cheating. It was the only possible answer.

At the teacher's urging, the vice principal called me into his office and searched all my stuff. They went through my backpack and my books. They didn't find anything, and I'm not sure what they expected to find.

The teacher stood there and said, "There's no way this kid could ace every test when he's sleeping most of the time in class."

I don't remember the tone he used, but in my head it sounded like this: "There's no way *this* kid could ace every test when he's sleeping most of the time in class."

Since the search didn't work as expected—they didn't uncover any cheat sheets or answers written on the inside of my eyelids—they came to their second conclusion: I was on drugs.

The day after the search, the teacher marched me back into the vice principal's office. The teacher and I sat down on the other side of the desk.

"You must be smoking weed or something at lunch because you keep falling asleep in class," the vice principal said.

The teacher was nodding along. I didn't give them the satisfaction of a response. I didn't defend myself or discuss my epilepsy medication because I just didn't care anymore. I knew school wasn't for me, and I knew my wild streak of independence wouldn't allow me to play by rules written up by officious pricks like these guys. Besides, I was doing enough drugs to make their assumptions plausible.

They knew I had epilepsy. The school nurse had my pills in case I needed them. The teacher was frustrated because he couldn't believe I could do the work without hanging on his every word.

Here's one of my problems with the educational system: It never occurred to this teacher or this vice principal to look into it any deeper. Why couldn't they test me, or interview me, or see if maybe I was different? It didn't fit into their worldview that I might be a fuckup *and* a math genius. Maybe I had a capacity to do the work that had nothing to do with paying attention to him. The vice principal didn't like me because I was always getting into trouble. I *was* a bad kid and I did do bad things. I wasn't an angel, no doubt, but it was demoralizing when they couldn't even acknowledge that I was good at something. I had a talent for math and reasoning, but they couldn't see it through the tangle of assumptions caused by my overall poor behavior. Partly my fault, partly theirs. There's no debating the end result, though: I hated school and didn't see much point to it.

The solution? They dropped me to a lower-level math class. How's that for education? Kid whizzes through an advanced math class, gets demoted because the teacher can't figure him out. Perfect.

My new math teacher was Mr. White. I think I remember the names of three teachers in my storied academic career, and Mr. White is one of them. He was one of the very few African-American teachers at Taft, and he was cool. I'd been in his class for about two weeks when he asked me to stay after for a one-on-one conversation.

Everyone left the classroom. I walked up to his desk, not knowing what to expect but bracing myself for the worst. It was easier that way, since I was usually right.

"Listen," Mr. White said. "You're a really bright kid. You've got no business in this class."

He was right. I had no business in his class. The problem was, I didn't think I had any business in any class.

HOW BAD OF A kid was I? By the time I was in eighth grade, I had tried every drug imaginable. I took phenobarbital for my epilepsy and everything else for the sheer hell of it. If someone had it, I tried it. I guess it was all part of my fatalistic approach to life. If you're going to die anyway, why not make the most of the days you have? Right or wrong, that was my attitude.

Oh, and there was this: I stole my dad's motor home. I was fourteen.

I hatched a scheme where I would take the motor home, pick up two of my neighborhood friends, and drive to Las Vegas.

It was going to be a great time. There wasn't a lot of forethought given to the plan. We weren't really considering what our parents would think when they realized we were gone. We weren't really considering that it might be obvious that we were gone *and* the motor home was gone.

It's difficult to sneak away in a motor home.

We tried anyway. The idea was to leave in the evening, I guess to provide the cover of darkness. I started the motor home up and drove about three blocks to pick up the buddy who lived closest. I parked the motor home a couple doors down and went to his house.

At this point, we were all systems go. I hung out in my buddy's house for a while, waiting for him to secretly pack a few things and get out of the house without drawing too much suspicion.

Well, it took longer than we expected, and when we got to the motor home—all full of bad-kid anticipation and adrenaline—we were in for a surprise. I had left the lights on, and the battery was dead. So was our plan.

I had to go back home and explain to my parents about their motor home. Awkward, to say the least, not just for the scheme but for the stupidity of leaving on the lights. More broadly, this was sort of a watershed moment for me. It left my parents with no choice but to realize just how thoroughly evil and horrible I was. Certain things could be excused or ignored as boys-will-be-boys, but a fourteen-year-old stealing a motor home with the intent of taking two of his buddies more than three hundred miles to Las Vegas was more than even distracted parents could ignore.

Whatever lecture they gave me, whatever words of wisdom Old Man imparted upon the jump-starting and return of the Winnebago, it didn't work.

It probably wasn't more than a few weeks after that episode when a couple of friends and I downed a fifth of Southern Comfort at lunch. I was so drunk—passed-out drunk, in fact—I left the administration at Taft Middle School with no option but to warehouse me in the nurse's office and call my parents.

When my parents picked me up, they didn't take me home. Instead, they took me to the Southwind Mental Health Center, an inpatient drug and alcohol rehab center for teenagers.

My parents didn't know what else to do with me. They knew they couldn't control me, and they knew the school couldn't control me, and they'd come to the conclusion I couldn't control myself.

So I was a fourteen-year-old in rehab. I left eighth grade to go to rehab. If you can look at this picture and see the makings of a successful businessman and television personality, you've got better vision than I do.

I went straight from the school to the rehab center. I didn't argue or fight; I was too drunk for that. I had no idea where I was or what was happening. It's obvious my parents had been contemplating a move like this for some time, because they had the intake people all set to admit me when we arrived.

Once I came to my senses, later that night, I was pissed off. I didn't believe that I was a drug addict. I rationalized it like every person in that situation: Most of my use was during the weekends, I didn't stick to one drug, I didn't often spend my lunch break sucking down SoCo behind a building. It was the seventies, it was the drug culture, I was just one of those assholes who wanted to try everything. One weekend it was acid, the next it was weed, the one afterward it was quaaludes. No harm, no foul.

(I was scared shitless of needles, so I never went there. I dreaded the monthly visits to get my blood drawn at the military hospital. Sometimes it took fifteen pokes for them to tap into the right vein. Eventually I started pointing to a trustworthy vein and saying, "Right there. That one right there," whenever the nurse entered the room.)

My new living arrangement put a crimp in my primitive life plan, which was to do whatever the hell I wanted for as long as I wanted. That might not be that long anyway.

The most amazing revelation of being in a drug treatment facility came when I realized I could buy drugs in there. I was scoring weed in rehab, at an AA meeting they held inside the building.

The second revelation came from the teachers, who started telling me I was one of the smartest kids they'd ever been around. I don't say this to brag, but their words changed my life. The facility included a school, where we took classes in the mornings and attended meetings and group sessions the rest of the day.

These teachers were the first ones who saw me without judgment. I was in a drug treatment center as a fourteen-year-old, so they knew I was a troubled kid. They knew I was a fuckup, so they weren't really trying to figure out what was wrong with me. My presence indicated a tacit understanding that I needed some help.

The teachers at Taft just wanted to know why I was disruptive and asleep and getting 100 percent on tests I didn't appear to care about. Here, the 100 percent I got on tests was seen in a different light. Inside rehab, my brain was seen as a great thing. *Hey, everybody. This kid might be troubled, but he's a goddamned genius.*

These teachers were the first people who didn't search for reasons why I might not be as smart as I appeared. They saw me as someone who spent five minutes doing his work and the rest of the time twiddling his thumbs and staring at the walls while everyone else sweated out every problem.

They encouraged me. That was a first, too. They allowed me to spend the last ten or fifteen minutes of every class period trying to teach the other students how to do complicated math problems in their heads. I didn't have great success, but the process gave me a level of self-confidence I didn't have previously.

Also, the program ran on a points system. The more points you accumulated—through good behavior or schoolwork or a good deed— the more freedom you were afforded. So I told my math teacher, "I'll do a week's worth of homework today if it means more points for me." She was good with that, and almost immediately I was racking up points faster than they could count them.

After three months, I transitioned out of the inpatient treatment facility and into a six-month day school that was the outpatient part of the program. I was given an assessment test on the first day, and I scored 100 on the math. After it was graded, they told me the test topped out at third-year college math. I was fourteen.

"The way these results look, you're a genius when it comes to math," the lady running the program told me.

I didn't argue. I had thought I was a math genius since fifth grade, when I thought I'd discovered differential squares. I wasn't aware that someone else had discovered the concept many, many years before me. I was messing around with numbers because I enjoyed it, and eventually I stumbled upon this way of figuring out 59 cubed in your head by using squares.

The self-confidence I gained in rehab was great, but there was also a dark side. You tell a fourteen-year-old kid like me that he's a genius, you're asking for problems. A little tip: It's probably the worst thing you can tell him, even if it is true. I was already a bad kid, full of evil thoughts and vile schemes. I was willing to do anything that sounded fun or cool or adventurous.

Now I was being told I was a genius?

Uh-oh.

Bad move.

I became a bad kid who was even cockier than before. I was arrogant, which meant there was no chance I was going to listen to anybody. This was all the evidence I needed that I was smarter than the adults in my life.

And imagine the look on my parents' faces when the teacher from the reform school told them the news. They were dealing with me on a certain level: wild, undisciplined, and nearly impossible to reason with. I was an epileptic who required a lot of extra care. I was the source of a lot of worry on many different fronts.

Again, a puzzle.

I was in eighth grade, capable of doing college-level math. But I was also doing third grade–level spelling. I couldn't spell to save my life, and I think it was because it made no mathematical sense to me. Why isn't "school" spelled s-k-o-o-l?

Math made sense. Math fit the concept of order, and spelling didn't. Spelling was arbitrary, the product of someone's whims.

I never was big on trusting anyone but myself.

I'D LIKE TO SAY spending three months in a locked rehab facility changed my outlook on life, but I was too young for any lasting transformations. There were a lot of complicated thoughts floating through my immature brain, and three months was not enough time to get them all sorted out. I was an invincible kid who was haunted by mortality. I was a fatalist who lived like I was bulletproof.

Three months of lockup helped me develop some self-esteem. I walked out knowing I was not just a kid who always seemed to make the wrong choices. I was smart, and smart could be cool. The kids and teachers who followed my in-your-head math lessons were quite amazed at my facility with numbers.

And I filed some valuable information away in my head for later use. I might not have been ready to drop my bad-boy lifestyle completely, but in realizing a few things about myself I couldn't help but be improved in the process.

I didn't do as much drugs. I stopped smoking weed after I realized what an idiot it made of me. I didn't steal any more motor homes. I didn't get hammered on SoCo at lunch at school anymore.

School was a problem I solved in a different way: I quit going.

I finished eighth grade in the facility. Back at Taft, ninth grade was a different story. I left the house in the morning like I was going to school, but I just took a little detour and hitched a ride to San Diego's Mission Beach. It was pretty easy, really: I spent my whole ninth grade year at the fucking beach and nobody said boo.

Eventually, I went back and finished ninth grade, but that was the pinnacle of my formal education. I didn't stop learning, though. I see it as a trade: I went from being taught by teachers to being taught by the world around me.

VEGAS DREAMING

**ACK IN 1973, WHEN I WAS EIGHT YEARS** old, my dad bought a brand-new Volkswagen Thing. If you've ever seen a Volkswagen Thing, you're probably questioning the wisdom of that decision. However, setting aside the aesthetics of the vehicle, my dad's purchase of the 1973 Volkswagen Thing had a big impact on my life.

Why? Because I was there. I was in the showroom with him, and it was the first time in my life I ever watched someone negotiate.

It was a civil conversation between my dad and the salesman for the longest time. I wasn't really paying attention, because at the time it was just two adults doing their adult talk. The salesman was doing most of the talking, and my dad was listening patiently and occasionally asking a question. It was clear the salesman felt he was on his game, and he definitely seemed to be in charge of the conversation.

But then, without warning, the volume rose and the tone changed. My dad raised his voice, and it caught everybody in the room off-guard. The salesman gathered his bearings and came back at my dad, which really set Old Man off. He got furious with this guy, yelling and jabbing his finger in the air at him. He was going on and on until people were coming out of their offices to see what was causing all the commotion.

The salesman, clearly flustered, walked away from my dad and said something about having to talk to his manager. "We'll get this settled, Mr. Harrison," he said. His calm was gone, his mojo shattered. He was no longer in charge of the conversation. It was clear the power dynamic in the relationship had shifted.

"I'll talk to my manager and be right back," the salesman said.

"You do that," Old Man said.

My eyes must have been as big as basketballs during this tirade; I was staring at my dad and wondering what could have made him that mad that quickly. I was feeling sorry for the salesman, because it didn't seem as if he'd done anything to set my dad off. And as the salesman turned his back and walked away, my dad turned to me and gave me a big wink.

It took me a second before I realized what was happening. *It was all a game.* My dad wasn't really mad at this guy; he was just doing what he had to do to get himself the best deal. I remember feeling relieved that it wasn't going to end up in a bloody fistfight, and then I thought to myself, *Ah, so* that's *how this works. It's all for show.*

The episode in the Volkswagen dealership is something I think about often. It was a memory that gained significance as the years went on. Not only did I learn something about negotiation, but I realized that a business transaction is not meant to be a friendship. The salesman wanted to be my dad's friend, but for my dad the purchase of a 1973 Volkswagen Thing wasn't a sentimental endeavor. He knew what he wanted, and he knew what he wanted to pay for it. End of story. Anything beyond that, including the salesman's feelings, was immaterial.

Even though I wasn't allowed to play sports, I was always a fiercely competitive kid who needed to find an outlet for that competitiveness. Watching my dad and that salesman, I realized something: *That was a competition.* And since we ended up bringing The Thing home with us, I knew Dad got the better of that slick salesman. Say what you will about a 1973 Volkswagen Thing, but it was proof of his victory.

The Thing ended up having a long and colorful life in our family. It made the trip with us from San Diego to Las Vegas, and it ultimately ended up being driven by both of my brothers and me. My older brother, Joe, did some damage to it before it was passed along to me. I fixed it up a little bit and worked on it to get it going, and one night I was driving down the freeway at about midnight and . . . *whoosh!* . . . the roof ripped clean off and flew down the freeway behind me. So for about the next few months I drove a car without a roof—or a heater—in the winter in Las Vegas, where it gets colder than you might think, especially at night.

But while the history of The Thing might be irrelevant, its place in my memory is strong. It represented the first time I saw firsthand the power of negotiation, and the first time I discovered that prices were only suggestions, not absolutes.

THE MONEY BUG HIT me for good when I was twelve. When people ask when I began working for my dad, I say it started then, when he started taking me to swap meets on Saturday mornings to look for overlooked treasures and, believe it or not, silver spoons. Those aren't just a cliché, by the way. Up until the 1980s, you could forage through swap meets and garage sales and pick through people's stuff to find silver spoons. When people sell silverware, the everyday stuff often gets mixed up with Grandma's old silver collection. It might be one out of five hundred, but if you took your time and knew what you were looking for, you could come away with some pretty good finds. It wasn't unusual for us to find ten spoons over the course of a weekend.

My dad always sold gold and silver, subscribing to the idea that metals are a surefire investment. Gold has a hallowed place in the eyes of American investors. There's a historical reason why so many people retreated to gold during the mortgage meltdown and banking crisis. In 1933, during the banking crisis after the Great Depression, President

Franklin D. Roosevelt signed Executive Order 6102, which required U.S. citizens to turn in their gold. It prohibited citizens from owning more than $100 worth of gold coins. This limitation on gold ownership was not fully rescinded until President Gerald Ford signed a bill in 1974. Because of this, gold has become the investment of choice among those who either fear or distrust the government, and the sheer quantity of people with those beliefs caused the price of gold to spike to more than $1,300 an ounce in 2010.

And now back to my childhood: Searching for treasure at garage sales and swap meets was a pastime that required a great deal of patience, and even though I was a wild kid, I found I had the patience and determination to pick through the chaff in search of the wheat. I was very focused, a fact I attribute to the hours spent on my bed reading all day with the ice packs on my legs.

My lifelong curiosity and quest to determine real from fake started simply: with my dad teaching me the difference between real and fake silver. He taught me to examine everything very closely, and it gave me a feeling of power to pull a real silver spoon out of the pile.

Since he grew up with nothing and didn't like the feeling, my dad has always been a hustler, the kind of guy who would learn about something and use it for his own benefit and profit. Old Man's always had a combination of curiosity and savvy. He's got street smarts and an uncanny ability to read people.

I had spent most of my life either ignoring or disobeying my parents, but our new partnership was cool. Everything was new, everything was different. There was so much to learn, which appealed to my analytical side. My mom got interested, and roaming swap meets for hidden treasure became something the three of us could do together. (Funny, they weren't overly involved parents when it came to school, but they were happy to spend time with me when there was money to be made.) If I wasn't spending the weekend helping my dad fix up his run-down rental houses in San Diego, I was hanging out at swap meets and garage sales.

During this time, I was still having seizures, but they were starting to become less and less frequent. You might have an image of me as an aimless, drug-addled kid, but I had a passion for things that interested me. I was taking semiregular trips to the public library, and in my readings on epilepsy I came to conclude that my seizures were changing from grand mal to petit mal. They weren't as ferocious, and they weren't as frequent. I could almost feel my heart bounce in my chest when I read that oftentimes kids my age simply grew out of the seizures and no longer had to take medication.

It was difficult for me to find the kind of comprehensive information on epilepsy that would satisfy my fierce need for knowledge. This wasn't the age of the Internet, of course, so I couldn't simply log into WebMD and go to town. I had to find medical journals or textbooks that might provide an overview of the disease or give me some little tidbits—like the information about the evolution from grand mal to petit mal.

This was important, because I was getting to the age where I could see a huge milestone looming: a driver's license. This wasn't going to happen as long as I was still having seizures; I knew for a fact the state of California wasn't going to issue me a driver's license if I was an active epileptic.

So, starting before my fifteenth birthday, I took matters into my own hands.

I told my parents I'd stopped having seizures.

This lie was easier to tell because they were becoming far less frequent and far less severe. The petit mal seizures were no picnic, but they were far less traumatic than the full-blown grand mal. However, just as I started to lose my fear that a massive grand mal seizure was going to kill me, another concern began.

Sitting in front of the television one night, the world went black. My eyes were open, but it was as if a black curtain had been pulled over my eyes. I sat there, half-expecting a seizure to follow, but nothing happened. I tried not to panic, and I tried not to let anyone know there was a chance I was going blind. After a period of time—probably fifteen to thirty seconds—my vision returned as quickly as it had left.

These bouts of blindness happened periodically over a stretch of about six months. Terrified of not being able to get my license, I kept quiet about them. This wasn't the wise choice, of course, but the truth was they scared the hell out of me and I believed there was a chance they would stop if I just wished them away.

Every time my sight returned at the end of one of these episodes, I felt like a miracle had happened. And then, just like the seizures, the bouts of blindness became less frequent and less severe, until they ultimately went away entirely. I never investigated what caused them, probably because I was in denial. It was almost as if I willed them out of my life.

Sixteen was a big year for me. My last seizure came when I was sixteen. The bouts of blindness came and went when I was sixteen. I got my driver's license when I was sixteen.

I hadn't had a seizure for quite some time when the last one hit. I'm embarrassed to admit it happened after I had ingested four or five quaaludes. I'm guessing I might have brought that one on myself.

Yeah. Smart, huh? I might have been a genius, but that didn't stop me from doing stupid things.

NOBODY COULD FIGURE ME out. I was a tenth-grade dropout who read and studied more than most college students. I could be a raging, partying guy on Friday night and then get up Saturday morning, pack three or four physics books into a backpack, hop on a motorcycle, and drive into the desert. I'd sit on the side of a mountain all day long reading them. No wonder nobody knew what to make of me. I wasn't always sure, either.

When I was fifteen, I got my hands on a copy of Isaac Asimov's *Un-*

derstanding Physics. You would have thought I'd found a new drug. I read that thing front to back three times, one after another. I eventually got all four volumes and read through them the way some people shred through Harry Potter books. To me, it was not only educational, it was fascinating, and it was fun. To this day, I love to read physics books, and I will not apologize for that.

The bottom fell out of my parents' real estate business when I was sixteen. All I can remember them talking about was the high interest rates—as high as 18 percent—and the complete shutdown of the housing market. They started losing money, until they didn't have any more money to lose.

One day my dad came into the family room to talk to me and my two brothers.

"Sons, we're moving to Las Vegas," he said. "We just can't make a go of it here anymore."

He was never much of a talker, or an explainer, but he outlined what he wanted to do. He would go to Vegas because Vegas was the best place to start a small business buying and selling coins and jewelry.

Looking back on it, it was a desperation move. They waited out the real estate market and figured it wasn't bouncing back anytime soon, thanks to the 18 percent interest rates. My dad had his navy pension and his smarts, and I'm sure there was a big part of him that relished the challenge of making a new life for himself by surviving on his business savvy and his wits.

So we picked up and moved. I was sixteen. It would have been a rough time for most kids to do this, but since I wasn't in school it was a little less of an upheaval for me. It was tough to leave my friends, guys I'd hopped fences at Jack Murphy Stadium with, devised plans to steal motor homes and drive to Vegas with, done drugs with. But to be honest, for a guy with an interest in moneymaking and an absolute love for the wonder of our crazy world, Vegas was a great place.

My parents had about five grand to their name when they moved, and my dad immediately opened his little buy-and-sell store on Las Vegas Boulevard. He did OK, well enough to stay in business but not well enough to ever take a single day off. He worked day and night to get that shop started, and eventually it began to pick up.

Las Vegas is a hustler's paradise. There's always something going on, with people buying and selling, yard sales and auctions, gamblers flush with cash and gamblers down to their last dime. There's always a deal to be made, and my old man is the ultimate deal-maker. He didn't know how this new chapter of his life was going to work, but he knew that he had to provide for his family and that failing at this was not an option. So, like all workaholic men of the Depression and post-Depression era, he worked his ass off in that place to make sure he—and we—would make it.

A LOOK BACK AT my employment history reveals some of the strangest jobs known to man: repo man, mall-kiosk gold-chain salesman, paddle-tire entrepreneur, motorcycle-chain salesman, payday-advance guy, pawnbroker.

In my late teens I got a job selling these chains in the mall. They called the kiosk Hitch of Gold, and it was a big deal for a long time. They were layered, fake gold chains that came with a lifetime warranty. We sold the chain for twenty bucks. To get the lifetime warranty, all you had to do was fill out a form and send it in the mail with five bucks for shipping and handling.

Guess what? It was the world's greatest scam. This was the beginning of the bling era, I guess, when even white suburban kids started feeling like they could pull off jewelry. High school kids bought these little chains faster than the factory could churn them out. The best part: The chain cost a buck to produce, one-fifth of the warranty. I made some good money as a teenager off that job.

But most of my time was spent working with my dad. The shop did well enough that we wanted to expand.

We had no idea about politics. We walked into this—owning a shop, living in Vegas—completely clueless about the ins and outs of city politics. If we wanted to take the jump from secondhand store to pawn shop, we needed to upgrade our Class 3 license to an unlimited one. That was a much bigger task than getting the Class 3 had been.

This became my dad's dream: to own a pawn shop in Vegas. At this point, in the late 1980s, most of the pawn shops in town were being bought up by huge corporations like EZPAWN and PawnAmerica. The mom-and-pop pawn shop was becoming obsolete in Vegas, which is probably the most lucrative pawn market in the world. But my dad loved competition and never backed down from a challenge. More on that later.

WHEN I WAS SEVENTEEN, I got my girlfriend Kim pregnant. This was one of those life moments that define who you are as a person. We didn't want to be in this position, trust me. We were both immature, content to run around Vegas partying and goofing off like we didn't have a care in the world. Which we didn't, until the day Kim came to me and told me she was pregnant. Then we had more than we could count.

I went to Kim and her family and said the right thing to do was to get married, so we would get married. Everyone agreed, but before the plan could be put into action—before I could "do the right thing" as it were—Kim miscarried.

We got married anyway.

What can I say? It was on our minds, it was already a plan, so by the time we got the sad news of the miscarriage we decided we'd go ahead and go through with it. We got married and resumed our partying, carefree ways, until we got news after about two months of marriage that Kim was pregnant again.

We were eighteen when Corey was born. As I saw him and the reality of an entirely new life ahead of me, I changed the way I lived. I don't know if being a dad scared me or inspired me—probably a little of both—but the whole idea of "Dad" injected me with this overwhelming sense of responsibility. I decided to quit being an idiot, which meant stopping the drugs and the consistent partying. This was a new phase of my life—call it the beginning of The Adult Phase—and even though it started a little earlier than I would have liked, I understood the significance and was ready to accept it.

Corey and I were always tight, from the day he was born. And within two years, Kim and I had another boy, Adam, and the three of us always managed to find a way to have a good time, even when we didn't have much money.

Kim and I had different approaches to parenting, so there was some tension in the marriage. We were young, stupid, and having kids. It wasn't an ideal situation. We were trying to make it on our own, and making it up as we went along. I worked for my dad and tried to hustle for money on my own, but this was back when we had the little shop. Money was tight.

Among the many things I did to make extra money: repo cars. I worked at the shop during the day and repossessed cars at night. I'm an adrenaline junkie. I love driving fast and bombing around the desert in my all-terrain vehicles. Repo work was one of the most exciting things I ever did. It was a rush.

During this time, there were used car lots all over town that had signs all over. "We'll Finance You." "No Money Down." Three weeks after they didn't get a payment, they're calling me with a list. Get this car. Get that car.

These were low-rent operations—the street term was "slut lots"—that couldn't afford a tow truck. But slut lots being slut lots, they always made a spare set of keys, just in case. I'd go into the lot's office and get my marching orders: sets of keys and a list of addresses.

You know how they ask you for a list of close friends or relatives when you fill out the paperwork for buying a car? Well, that's not for credit purposes or character references. They need those addresses in case you don't make the payments and they need to repo the car. Those were the addresses they handed me along with the keys. If the car wasn't at the owner's house, I'd move to the next address. They figure if you're not at home, there's a good chance you'll be at your mom's house, or at the house of one of your two best friends.

And there was always the work fallback. They always know where you work, so if we couldn't find the car at one of the listed addresses, we'd go to the buyer's place of employment. I've never had so much fun as I had sneaking into gated employee parking lots, finding a car, and watching the gate swing open as I drove out. Those were good times.

KIM AND I SEPARATED shortly after Adam was born. It could have been our immaturity combined with the pressures of having two kids at such a young age, but we couldn't make it work. After the breakup, I was a typical twenty-year-old living in Vegas—dating occasionally but not seriously—with one exception: I was focused on raising my two little boys.

I was always busy, but it was the good kind of busy. No matter how bad the day was, the boys were always glad to see me and we always managed to find ways to have fun. There was a lot of uncertainty in my life—financially and emotionally—but my commitment to the boys grounded me.

Jumping into another serious relationship was about the furthest thing from my mind, but fate has a way of messing with plans. Eight or nine months after Kim and I broke up, I met a nice girl from West Virginia named Tracy.

We met on a blind double date. One of my friends was dating Tracy's cousin, and the two of them decided Tracy and I should get together. This happened to take place during one of my least impressive stretches as a human being. For one thing I was struggling to raise two little boys, and I was broke, too. I literally did not have a dime to my name. For another, I was driving a car that refused to go into reverse. And as it happens, my car was deemed the most reliable transportation for this first date.

I was clearly not much of a catch, but I came into the date with my usual swagger, knowing I was carrying the one weapon that could make up for all the others: the gift of gab. I always had it, and I was never afraid to use it. In this case, I needed it more than ever.

Without money—my buddy was as broke as I was—or a car that could back up, planning for this date took some ingenuity. Where do you go and what do you do if money can't be part of the equation? Fortunately, Vegas is the best place in the world to entertain without money.

My buddy and I picked up Tracy and her cousin, and I know how stupid this sounds but it's true: I fell in love the second she stepped into the car. I'd been dating girls or just hanging out with them in the months since my divorce, and I was enjoying my second bout with the single life. As I said, the idea of jumping into a serious relationship was the last thing on my mind—until I saw her.

I've always been able to talk my way through situations. I can bullshit with the best of them, whether it's talking to a customer or a potential girlfriend. In this case, given my financial situation and my immediate feelings for Tracy, I had my work cut out for me.

We drove to the Stardust. The parking lot, like all casino lots, was big enough that I could drive way out past all the other cars and find a stall in the middle of nowhere. I didn't tell them why, and neither Tracy nor her cousin asked.

So far, so good. We went into the keno lounge and that's when I let Tracy know I had zero money to spend on her that night.

"OK, here's the deal," I said. "I'm broke, so we're going to sit here in the lounge, order drinks and act like we're playing keno."

I don't know how impressed she was, but she was a good sport and played along. We got a few hours of entertainment out of that—for nothing—and then headed back to the car. As we're walking through acres and acres of asphalt, I'm looking at the car up ahead. My stomach sinks.

"There is no way—no fucking way," I said.

Yes, there was a way. There had been one car in the middle of nowhere in the Stardust lot; now there were two. And the second one, of course, was in the space directly opposite my no-reverse car.

My buddy started howling with laughter. I was not so amused.

So that secret got thrown into the open.

I looked at my buddy, shrugged, and said, "OK, I guess it's Freddy Flintstone."

He got in the passenger side and I put it in neutral. We kicked the car back far enough that I could get it started and drive forward.

Even though I didn't have a whole lot going for me, Tracy accepted my offer for a second date. And a third. We dated for about six months before she moved in with me. She jumped right in, helping with the boys and becoming Instant Mom. Just add kids. She was wonderful from the start, and the boys accepted her into their lives like she'd always been there. After eight more months, we were married.

It didn't take long after that for Corey and Adam to start calling Tracy "Mom." They first started doing it because it was easier to explain to their friends, and eventually they called her that because she *was* their mom.

Kim showed up and said she wanted the kids back. That, as you might expect, didn't go over very well in my household. I'll just say it didn't happen and leave it at that.

Kim became the good-time weekend person, which created its own set of problems. This situation wasn't unique—although usually it's the father who's the good-time weekend guy—but all the discipline fell to us. It was hard for Tracy to be the one who had to get them to school, tell them to do their homework, and get on them when they pushed back.

As it turned out, Corey became a real mama's boy. Up until a year before he got married, he was bringing his dirty laundry over to our house every Sunday for Tracy to wash. He was twenty-four years old, and I told Tracy, "You don't have to do this if you don't want to. I can tell him to stop coming over."

I even needled him. "You're a grown man. She doesn't need to be doing your laundry anymore."

Tracy would interrupt me. "Don't you dare," she'd say. "I want him to come over. I like doing it."

It wasn't the laundry she enjoyed; it was getting a chance to talk to him every week and give him advice on the kind of life issues guys just don't talk about with other guys. Corey might tell you he was there because he needed clean clothes, but I think he might have been there for the conversation, too.

For one thing, her advice was solid. Corey dated a girl named Charlene when they were in middle school, but they went their separate ways for several years. During those years, when Corey was dating a million girls, mostly strippers, Tracy would tell him repeatedly, "You need to meet a nice girl like Charlene."

Eventually, when he was about twenty-three, Corey got back together with Charlene. They dated for a little more than a year and got married.

See? Tracy was right. I don't know how many times she mentioned Charlene, and I don't know whether her suggestions subliminally got into Corey's head, but I know this much: Tracy isn't doing Corey's laundry anymore.

THE HARD WAY

I **TELL PEOPLE THE BEST THING ABOUT** running a family-owned business is working with my family. I also tell them the worst thing about running a family-owned business is working with my family. Most guys my age talk to their dad a few times a week, and if they live in the same community they might see each other once or twice a week. Maybe they meet on a Sunday afternoon to watch a ball game or something.

Here's another way we're different: Guys my age are usually able to call their dad and vent about work. OK . . . you think I can do that? Or, by the same token, do you think my son, Corey, can do that?

My deal is pretty unusual. Old Man and I see each other every day, usually for eight or nine hours a day, and then we have to look at each other on holidays, too. I love him, and I feel so bad for all the stuff I put him and my mom through during my childhood. That's why it's so great that we can share this success, both in the shop and on television, together.

I tell Old Man this to his face, so it's no secret. I'm heartened by the fact that I know he feels the same way about me. And you know what? I'm sure Corey does, too. We're all in this together, which doesn't mean we always have to agree, or be happy to see each other.

Old Man will never stop working. I honestly think he'd be dead within six months of walking out that door. He and my mom love each other and would do anything for each other, but there's no way they could coexist in the same house all day long with nothing to do but talk and watch television. My mom's got some serious health problems, diabetes primary among them, and she's in a wheelchair. Sometimes Old Man just wants to get the hell out of the house.

My mom has a caretaker, so it's not like he's leaving her by herself, but he just gets stir crazy. Plus, he's a hopeless workaholic. That's his vice. He doesn't go out. I bet he can't remember the last time he went into a bar and had a drink with friends. Me? There are probably twenty bars in this town that I can walk into and have the bartender say, "What's up, Rick?" And that was true before people recognized me from the television show.

Anyway, Old Man is like a lot of guys from his generation: workaholics who can't bear the thought of not working. This is a man who has not taken a sick day since 1994. He worked seven days a week to get the shop going. As I said earlier, he's such an old soul he earned the nickname "Old Man" when he was just thirty-eight years old.

There are a million Old Men out there in America right now. There are guys who retire from the insurance business who continue to go into the office just to make sure everything's working OK. There are guys in every walk of life who do the same thing my dad does, but the difference is he can get away with it because it's a family business and he still has something to offer.

Sometimes I'm the bad guy, though. He'll be sitting around the house in the morning, drinking his coffee, and he'll tell my mom, "Well, I'm going into the shop. Rick tells me he needs me today."

This isn't true at all. I haven't told him anything—he just wants to get out of the house. So then my mom will call me and say, "Why are you working your father so hard?"

Now *that's* a great position in which to find yourself. I've got two choices, either rat out my dad or look like a guy who's forcing his sixty-nine-year-old father to slave away in the family business. See what I mean about working with my family?

(It's better than it used to be, though. Back when he had more energy, Old Man used to tell my mom, "Hon, I'm going to work." Then he'd come into the shop and tell me, "Listen to me and listen to me good: Your mother thinks I'm working today, but today I feel like playing poker all goddamn day. So if she calls, tell her I had to testify in court and I don't know when I'll be home.")

We're different. Old Man is the micromanager, the guy who doesn't understand why we have four or five different departments and forty-seven employees, the guy who still wants to know every single item and penny that goes in and out of the store. And here's the great part: The better we do and the more money we make, the more he frets. The swag business has created a whole new opportunity for him to worry. There are days when he'll walk around the office asking for hourly updates on how many T-shirts we're selling, how many Chumlee shot glasses and Big Hoss bobbleheads. I just want to tell him, *Dad, this is a good thing. It's something we never had before, so it's all gravy.* He can't help it, though.

I'm much more willing to delegate responsibilities and take a longer view at the overall direction of the shop. And Corey is now managing the store, taking on the everyday responsibilities of scheduling and inventory and all that. I'm more than willing to allow him to do that stuff; I'm content to sit back, have fun, and look forward to the next bizarre item that walks through the door.

THERE ARE ASPECTS OF running a family-owned business in Las Vegas that are like taking a graduate-level crash course in local politics. When we lost our lease on the space we rented for our secondhand store on Fremont Street, we had to go before the Las Vegas City Council to get approval to move into a new building on Las Vegas Boulevard. We expected it to be little more than a rubber stamp, since it was a commercial neighborhood and not an area where a secondhand store would be out of place.

However, there was one particular council member who was determined to become our nemesis. At the council meeting the night we were on the agenda, he went on a twenty-minute tirade why we shouldn't be allowed to move to Las Vegas Boulevard. He thought we'd be bad for the neighborhood—if you've been there, you know that's comical—and he went on from there. By the time he was finished, anyone listening would have believed that we stood for the worst of everything.

We were taken aback by this guy. We'd never met him, but he was vehement in his dislike for us. Old Man and I were looking at each other during the council meeting, thinking, *What is with this guy?* We started out in 1981 in a three-hundred-square-foot space—more like a room—on Las Vegas Boulevard South. We spent five years there before moving to a bigger space on Fremont Street. We were there for two years before losing our lease. We'd never had any problems at either location, so this was coming out of the blue.

The councilman's argument apparently swayed one voter, because we squeaked by 3–2 and got the go-ahead to move into the building we occupy today.

We were happy to move, no matter what our nemesis believed, and we didn't give him a second thought. (That's probably not entirely true, since I'm sure Old Man and I threw around some curse words in reference to him for a few weeks afterward.)

People like him represented minor setbacks, just more proof that we had to develop a tough hide to make it in this business in this city. From the beginning, my dad and I always had our eyes on a lucrative prize: one of Vegas's rare—and infrequently distributed—pawn licenses. It was the logical progression from coin shop to secondhand store to pawn shop. If we could get that license, there'd be no stopping us. The problem was, dreaming of owning a pawn shop in Vegas was the easy part. Getting a pawn license and actually setting up shop was the hard part.

I got on the phone to the city to see what it would take to get a license, and that's when I learned about an arcane 1955 law in the city of Las Vegas that called for pawn licenses to be sold based on the city's population. More specifically, one pawn license would be issued for every fifty thousand residents in the city.

Since the population at the time of my call was over two hundred thousand but below two hundred and fifty thousand, two-fifty became the number the city had to reach before we could get a license.

Clearly, we wouldn't be the only ones keeping tabs on that number. The big corporations would be fighting for the chance to add another store. There could be other independent pawnbrokers like us looking to get their hands on a license that figured to be as lucrative as this one.

My plan was simple: I would call the city statistician every single week to get an update on the population. Every Friday I'd make the call, and every Friday the same guy would give me the number. This was 1988, and Vegas was growing like crazy. One week it would be two hundred twenty nine thousand, the next week two thirty. I won't bore you with the details—it was just a guy calling another guy every Friday and getting a number for an answer, thanking him, and hanging up. Not exactly riveting dialogue.

Around this time, we had a surprise visitor walk through the door of the Gold & Silver Pawn Shop. It was none other than the honorable council member who'd run us down at the meeting.

Asking for a campaign contribution.

This is the guy who thought we were the worst thing that could ever happen to Las Vegas Boulevard, and probably Las Vegas itself. All smiles, he came in and shook my hand, looked me straight in the eye, and asked for money.

I was a smart-ass kid at the time, and I wasn't always the most tactful guy in the world. This time, though, I knew we had to swallow our pride—and our anger. This wasn't easy; I could feel Old Man breathing fire behind me. He was mumbling something. I was afraid he was going to come out of his chair and lunge at this guy's throat.

I tried to smile at the guy (it probably came out as a grimace), and I walked back to talk to my dad. He was staring me down, and I said, "You bite your fucking tongue. Give him some fucking money."

Old Man didn't want to hear this, but he knew it was the way the game was played. By this time, I had already started calling the city statistician for weekly updates on the population, with an eye on two hundred and fifty thousand and a pawn license. If we threw our council friend out of the shop by his ear, he'd make sure we never had a chance of realizing our dream and getting the city's next pawn license.

Worse still, he knew that, too. That's why he was in there.

I think we wrote him a check for a thousand bucks at a time when a thousand bucks meant a lot to us. He smiled and shook my hand again, thanked us for our contribution, and said he looked forward to doing business with us in the future.

I was still calling every week, and as the population got closer to two-fifty, I started calling every day. I had a picture of a meter running in my head, with the numbers rolling up like an odometer. I wanted to make sure I was on the phone with the statistician the second that thing rolled over from 249,999 to 250,000.

Then one day in early 1989, it happened.

Two-fifty.

I got off the phone and said, "Dad, he says it's two-fifty."

My dad didn't even look up.

"Then get your ass down there and get me my license."

Well, I did and I didn't. I got my ass down to the city business license office, ready to pay the $200 fee for the license, and said, "We've been told the city population is two hundred and fifty thousand, and I'd like to get the license."

Their answer was straightforward and stunning:

"No, we're not accepting those."

"Wait a second," I said. "The city population is two hundred and fifty thousand, and I'm the first one here. Give me my license."

"No."

No? Just no?

Apparently that was my answer: Just no.

We'd worked too hard to give up on this, so we got a lawyer right away and sent him down there to file a lawsuit. We eventually got ourselves in front of a judge, who reviewed the material, looked down from the bench, and said, "Mr. Harrison was the first person down there, get him a license."

That didn't work either. The city filed an appeal that included a clause that changed the licensing process. The new clause said I was now supposed to pay a $250,000 licensing fee. The judge looked at that and said, "No, you can't do that. You can't change the rules in the middle of the game."

By the third time they sent us back to the judge, he had lost his patience with the city manager and the city attorneys.

"If Mr. Harrison doesn't have a license by tonight," he said, "then you or one of your staff is going to be spending the night in jail tonight."

And that's how we got our license. It was probably the only way we were going to get the license, because they did not want to give it to us. They wanted to give it to one of the good ol' boys.

The city never anticipated that a twenty-five-year-old guy from an unimportant family would show up to claim the license. This was a valuable piece of paper, and people with more money and pull than me and Old Man—and that includes almost everyone—were determined to make sure we didn't get it.

We literally felt like we were fighting for our financial lives. We knew we were up against some powerful forces, but we also knew we were right. The license was rightfully ours. There was nothing in the city codes that said anything other than first-come, first-served when it came to the pawn license. We had completed the paperwork and had been approved, so it was our license.

We were working off 1955 laws that nobody had seen the need to change. The city had erupted in population and influence during that time, and the Las Vegas of 1989 was far more of a big city, and even a city with the corrupt origins of Vegas gets more corrupt the bigger it gets. When there's more at stake, there are more people to claim it. If the current movers and shakers had been able to foresee a scenario where father-and-son store owners would be in position to grab a lucrative pawn license from the hands of a big-time corporation, I'm sure they would have changed the laws long before the city's population hit two hundred and fifty thousand.

The license wasn't the final hurdle, though. Once the judge made his ruling, we had to go back before the city council for final zoning approval. On the night of the meeting, we didn't really know what to expect. We were so blindsided the last time, and this time there could have been another council member—or our friend again—who felt compelled to issue an impassioned tirade against us.

But lo and behold, when they got to our item on the agenda, who stands up and argues in our favor? Our old friend, that's who. The man who raged against us as being the worst thing that could ever happen to Las Vegas Boulevard spent fifteen minutes telling the city council that we were great ambassadors for Las Vegas and the most wonderful people on the damned planet, and the city would be crazy not to zone us for the pawn shop.

Ah, politics! How I love the civic-minded purity of those who serve the community.

*   *   *   *

WE STARTED THE SHOP with around $10,000 and the inventory on hand. The money was the hard part. We needed to have cash on hand to make more cash. If someone came to us with a Rolex and wanted to pawn it for $8,000 and we didn't have the cash on hand, he would go somewhere else and never come back. That's a customer you'll never have, and you don't know how many other people he might influence by bad-mouthing you and saying you don't have enough money to do the job.

Appearances matter in this business. (OK, you can laugh about this as you envision the crew of us behind the counter, but it's true.) We had to give off the impression that we were doing well even if we were struggling. No foreign businessman is going to walk into a pawn shop in Las Vegas with $50,000 worth of brand-new Rolex watches, looking for $25,000 in cash to gamble, and feel good if he looks across the counter and sees someone who looks like he can't afford his next meal. In fact, he's probably going to leave before he gets to the counter.

We did what we could to save and put everything back into the business. After we got the pawn license, for the first year Tracy and I lived in a small apartment with Corey and Adam, and I rode my bike to work. Whatever money we had was being loaned out. School clothes came late for a few years. If you start a pawn shop and you don't have much capital—and we didn't—there's a lot of danger.

It was constantly like this for ten years, with another consideration: the IRS. If you run a pawn shop and make $100,000 but loan out every last penny of it, the IRS doesn't give a damn. It didn't tell you to loan it out, so it still wants its $34,000. It was a grind. And loans weren't easy, either. The reputation of the pawn business works against us when we walk into a bank. Since it's against Small Business Administration rules to borrow money to lend it out to somebody else, we're out of luck when it comes to acquiring an SBA loan.

Tracy and I had a beat-up Volkswagen bus during the days when I was riding my bicycle to work. Tracy ferried the kids around while I pedaled my way down Las Vegas Boulevard. One day I started off to work but had to come right back because I forgot something. I ran into our apartment and left the bike out front for less than five minutes. When I got back, the bike was gone. If it wasn't bad enough that I had to ride a bike to work, now I'm staring at an empty spot where my bike stood five minutes earlier. I was *pissed*.

The next day—the very next day—I'm driving the Volkswagen bus to work and I see a fucking guy riding my bicycle. I said, "Well, you're fucked" and *boom!* I steered that bus right into the side of him, knocking him to the pavement.

I jumped out of the bus and walked up to him just in time to hear him say, "This looks like a lawsuit."

"Yeah, nice try, asshole."

I proceeded to let him know precisely why he was about to get a beating, and then I beat the shit out of him. When I felt he'd had enough, I tossed the bike into the back of the bus and drove to a Winchell's donut shop down the street, where I found a couple of cops having a cup of coffee. Yes, I went right to a Winchell's, and yes there were cops in there. I started talking a mile a minute.

"Hey, I just caught this guy who stole my bike. He's lying on the ground over there. Go arrest him."

The cops followed me there, but the thief wasn't there. I pointed the cops to the spot where he stole my bike. They looked down at the splotches of blood on the pavement. They looked up at me.

"Trust us," one of them said. "Looking at that red asphalt there, I don't think you want us to go pick this guy up."

I had to be satisfied with getting my bike back.

* * * *

WE FOCUSED EVERYTHING ON growing the pawn business, and sometimes that meant expanding beyond our core business. Old Man talked me into starting some payday loan shops as a means of diversifying our business. He had some experience with this type of lending back in his navy days, albeit in a less organized manner. Unfortunately, I hated every minute of it, and I felt slimy the whole time. It was a mess, truly predatory, and it felt like our prey consisted of people who were the least equipped to handle it. I know the pawn business has been vilified by Hollywood and elsewhere, but the pawn business is way more legitimate than the payday loan business. If there is a caste system in the underground economy, the payday loan businesses are bottom-dwellers. They provide a service by giving customers cash between paychecks. Their advertisements are geared toward making the consumer believe the stores are there to give them a temporary boost, to pay bills—or to use however—before their next check. The reality, however, is a bit more insidious; the parameters of the loans make it nearly impossible to pay back. Even though the business is legally allowed, morally it never felt right.

I started thinking of a better way of doing business. The interest rates at payday loan stores are as high as 1 to 2 percent *per day*. It's insane. People end up borrowing money they can never pay back. They pay the interest, over and over, and never get out from under the debt. It seemed like there had to be a better way of handling this.

So I came up with a business model that would change the rules of the game. The interest rates were still insanely high, roughly 60 percent, but that's just because it's an incredibly high-risk business. Instead of the exorbitant payday loan rate that compounds into infinity, I would loan you a hundred bucks with a $25 service fee and put you on a four-month payment plan. Once you'd completed your payments, you were good to go. I would actually work with the people and enable them to get out from under the debt load. My goal was to have them all pay their loans off so they'd come back for more loans, instead of making it nearly impossible for them to pay off their loans so I could continue to collect interest.

Well, some of the big boys in town didn't like what I was doing. By the time they started putting the screws to me, I had five stores, including one in a town north of Vegas that was managed by the husband of the madam at the local brothel. I was small compared to these corporate loan stores—both in business and cash reserves—so they started suing the hell out of me. They said I was stealing their employees. They said I was stealing their software. They said I was stealing their customer lists.

I went fuming to my lawyer every time. "This is bullshit," I'd say.

"You're right," he'd say. "But this is America, and you can sue anybody about anything at any time."

In one suit, they wanted copies of every loan I did—two thousand loans, twelve pieces of paper for each loan. That's twenty-four thousand pieces of paper, and they wanted certified copies at three bucks apiece. Seventy-two grand for paperwork. You get the idea? So if the guy has more money than you, you're going to get crushed.

And I got *crushed*.

In the end, I got out of the alternative-loan business. I sold out to the guy who was suing me—after a quarter million dollars in lawyers' fees.

I honestly think my business model for alternative loans would have worked better than the current payday-advance model. My ideas aren't born in a lecture hall in an Ivy League university, but I think some of them are pretty damned good.

Better, in fact, than a lot of the ideas that do come out of business school. From 1991 to 1999, Las Vegas had a used-car saleswoman as mayor. Jan Laverty Jones . . . oh, how I fought with her! She was glamorous, she was brilliant, she went to Stanford! We were all supposed to bow down to her status as the Queen of Las Vegas. Well, if you owned a pawn shop in Vegas, you remember her for one brilliant idea: Pawn Shop Mall.

That's right, she made a proposal to move all the pawn shops in Vegas to a Pawn Shop Mall on Industrial Park Road. This was a good idea because it would be better for all of us, she claimed, and we were supposed to relent in grateful supplication because Jan Laverty Jones went to Stanford and she hawked cars on TV for her husband's dealership chain. She knew what was best for us.

Pawn Shop Mall.

My response was typically direct: Are you fucking *high*?

I told the mayor's office, "OK, I'll agree to put all the pawn shops in a mall on Industrial Park Road as long as you agree to put all the grocery stores in a Grocery Store Mall right next door, and all the jewelry stores in a Jewelry Store Mall right next to that."

It was insane. It never became a reality, obviously, but the fact that we were forced to address such an issue was completely unbelievable. How could a proposal that wildly stupid even get past the first advisor before being shot down? Unbelievable.

Here's another example of bureaucracy in action: If you watch the show, you've undoubtedly noticed the palm trees in the median of Las Vegas Boulevard in front of the shop. Those were part of a beautification project the city did a few years ago in an attempt to make downtown Vegas easier on the eyes.

That's all well and good, but there used to be street parking before the median and the palm trees. The businesses along Las Vegas Boulevard, including ours, depended on those parking spots because they provided easy access, especially for our older customers.

When they came to me with the proposal, I said, "It's going to look beautiful when there are trees on the road next to a bunch of boarded-up buildings. If people can't park, they aren't going to shop there."

No matter. They did it anyway. And several of the shops along the road did close. I ended up buying the parking lot next to the shop as well as the building next door. The government building across the street, built a few years ago for the then-bustling Building Department, is now empty, too.

But you know what? Those palm trees sure do look nice on TV. I'll give the city that much.

DESPITE ALL THE STRUGGLES we had to get the business moving, there's no doubt we were extremely lucky to have gotten the pawn license when we did. Not only did we get in under 1955 laws, which call for us to pay only $200 every six months to retain our license, but we also benefited from the skyrocketing population of Las Vegas.

The process of obtaining a pawn license is much different now. The city still issues one pawn license every time the population rises by fifty thousand, but the current state of affairs—a drastically shrinking population—has rendered that temporarily moot. However, there is a lottery system in place that takes first-come, first-served out of the equation. Tickets are $200 apiece, and they routinely sell between two thousand and four thousand tickets, which means the city earns $400,000 to $800,000 from the lottery tickets alone. The lottery winner must pay the city $60,000 for the license, but that's still a bargain. The license is transferable, and people are willing to pay $1 million to get one. Our shop's license is zoned for Las Vegas Boulevard, so I could probably sell it for $2 million.

We got our license just as most family-run pawn shops were getting out. Like just about every business in America in the late eighties and early nineties, the pawn business was being overrun by corporate interests. Fewer and fewer companies were owning more and more shops.

The two big pawn corporations—PawnAmerica and EZPAWN—started eating up as many pawn shops as they could. By the time we had a foothold in the Vegas market, Gold & Silver Pawn was just one of two family-owned shops left in town.

This allowed us to be different. The corporate shops are limited in what they do. They cater to people who are pawning jewelry or other conventional, no-thought items. We wanted our shop to reflect our personalities: curious, knowledgeable, and eccentric. It would be boring if all we did was sell and pawn jewelry and lend out money. We wanted to focus on the rare and unusual. We were still going to do all the normal pawn-shop business, but we saw an opportunity to provide a service by inviting people to sell their rare and unusual items.

As it turned out, our desire to attract the more eccentric stuff happened organically. The guys working for a low hourly wage at EZPAWN aren't equipped to handle rare stuff, and their bosses don't want them trying.

If a guy has a $5,000 Gibson guitar and he *knows* he's got a $5,000 Gibson guitar, he's going to laugh at the guys at EZPAWN when they look at his guitar and offer him $400. He's going to walk out of there thinking they're fools. But if he comes to my place and deals with me, I'm going to do a couple of things: (1) appreciate the hell out of his $5,000 Gibson guitar, which is going to make him feel pretty good about himself and his decision to come to my shop; and (2) give him the respect he deserves for knowing he's got a cool item—one he probably doesn't want to give up—and deal with him as fairly as I can.

I'm probably going to end up giving that guy three grand for his guitar. And if he needs the money that week, he's probably going to take it and feel OK about it.

The other place isn't going to give him $3,000 even if they know a Gibson is worth $5,000. Remember, there are fake everything: fake Stratocaster guitars, and fake Gibsons, and there's no way in the world a guy at EZPAWN is going to know the difference between that guy's real one and a fake one. He's not trained to know, or paid enough to know, so he's going to pay the same $400 for a real or a fake. The risk of getting burned is just too great.

Believe me, if word got out that EZPAWN paid someone $3,000 for a Gibson guitar—even if it was real—they would be flooded with fake Gibson guitars and they probably wouldn't know the difference.

Well, I know the difference. Old Man knows the difference. Corey knows the difference. And I have the clientele that would be willing to pay the $5,000 I would be asking. That's the difference between me and the corporate shops.

So here's the way it shakes out: When one of the corporate shops is presented with something they don't recognize, or something that doesn't show up on their computer price sheet, they say, "I think you should take it to Gold & Silver Pawn."

Hey, that works for me.

ALL KINDS—AND THEN SOME

OUR SHOP IS A POOR PERSON'S BANK. This is probably the first fact you need to keep in mind when picturing the people who comprise our clientele.

Sure, we specialize in rare and unusual items, and the television show highlights the cool stuff we have and the people who bring it in. That's a part of our business, but it isn't a completely accurate portrait of the everyday back-and-forth inside the shop.

Who comes in the store? Just about everybody. There is the permanent degenerate class, which uses us to fund whatever sordid activities they're planning at the moment. They're generally harmless, eager to get whatever they can and get on with those sordid activities.

There are the collectors who are drawn to the rare and unusual. There are skylarkers who line up outside to wait for their turn to walk around the shop, take pictures, and buy a T-shirt with Chumlee's face on it.

Most of our customers, though, are hardworking people who live just outside the lines of what you might consider conventional American society. They're seasonal workers or itinerant construction workers or people who otherwise find themselves in Vegas in search of something they can't find anywhere else. And most of them were hit hard by the collapse of the economy.

Nevada was the state hardest hit by foreclosures, and Las Vegas was the worst place in Nevada. This is the absolute epicenter of The Great Recession. Unemployment went to almost 15 percent, the construction industry came to a halt, and tourism took a nosedive. This leaves a lot of people in trouble.

Here's an example of a ripple effect of the failing economy: I stopped buying tools or taking them on pawn. We were filling up the back room with expensive power tools, and nobody was buying them. And when I say nobody, I mean *nobody*. It got to the point where I couldn't give away power tools. There was simply no market for them.

When the economy was good, there was no stopping construction in Vegas. Guys were making good money in the building trades, and there was far more work than workers to do it. There was a joke that went along with it: The official bird of Las Vegas was the construction crane.

When the economy took a dive, workers who had been laid off were coming into the shop by the dozen—they had nowhere else to go. These guys might not have been real sharp at managing their money. They never thought it would run out, and God knows our schools don't do much when it comes to teaching financial responsibility. A lot of these guys were hoping to be able to get their tools back—the recovery was always just around the corner—but too often they never came back, and one day I looked around and we had about seventy-five saws in the back room. I would look at them and see more than lost tools; I would see broken dreams and a broken system. It's enough to make you heartsick, but if I kept on taking saws from down-and-out construction workers, I was going to end up just like them. My back room was starting to look like Home Depot.

One of the ways we can track the health of the economy is through the number of pawned items that remain in our back room for longer than 120 days without being picked up. The assumption is the people who pawned them couldn't come up with the original loan money, plus interest, to get the items back. These items "come off pawn," which means they are now the property of Gold & Silver Pawn, and ours to sell.

The numbers aren't definitive, but during a good economy—in this case, pre-2007—the recovery rate is roughly 90 percent. In the two or three years that followed the economic collapse, that rate dropped to roughly 80 percent. It's a statistically significant difference, but it also surprises people to know that eight out of ten items, even in the worst economic times, get picked up.

If there's one thing I've learned, it's that people will do what they have to do to make it work. It's amazing to me how resourceful people are when it comes to making a living and taking care of their families. There are hustlers out there who will simply find a way, regardless of the obstacles. There's a Hispanic guy I know who has raised six kids by going from pawn shop to garage sale to pawn shop, selling and pawning and working his way to a profit.

He has a system, and he has it down. He'll shop prices and ask me what I'd pay for something that he's seen in another store. Then he might pawn something with me and use the money to go make the purchase in the other store. Then he'll sell the item to me and use part of the profit to take his stuff off pawn.

Watching this guy work is enough to make anybody nervous. He's talking fast, asking questions, running the numbers through his head while he figures out his next move.

He's made his living this way for years. He's raised *six* kids doing it. It's not a hobby; it's a profession. There's not a big spread there, so he needs to be hustling full-time to make it. He's just one of the people I deal with who lives a little bit outside the typical American nine-to-five structure.

Here's a fact I'll bet most people don't realize: Roughly 25 percent of the adult population can't get a bank account. If you have bad credit, you can't get a bank account or a credit card. So what choices do those people have? They have me, and that's about it.

If you come to me with your big-screen television and pawn it for two hundred bucks, I'll charge you 10 percent a month—120 percent a year. I'll charge you a $50 storage fee and five bucks a month additional for storage. After 120 days, if you haven't picked it up, it comes off pawn and becomes mine.

People look at a 10 percent monthly interest rate and say, "You're gouging people." That would be true if this was a simple electronic trans-action, but it's anything but that. I've got to store your television—or painting or rare book or motorcycle—and five bucks a month isn't very much to pay for storage. Besides, this is the only place you can walk into and get a loan in exchange for your stuff with no questions asked.

Here's a scenario: A guy walks through my door with a new Rolex and wants to borrow five grand against it to go over to the Mandalay Bay and gamble. Clearly, he doesn't have five grand in his pocket or his bank account—or he doesn't have access to it at the moment. Providing I'm confident the Rolex isn't stolen, I'm going to take the watch, write him up a pawn slip, count out one-hundred-dollar bills until I get to five thou-sand, shake his hand, and send him on his way. I'm not going to ask him what he's going to do with the money, because frankly I don't care. He got something, I got something, and we're both clear on the terms of the transaction.

Now, change the location of the transaction from the pawn shop to a bank. The same guy walks through the door and says he wants to bor-row five grand.

"And, sir, what do you plan on doing with the money?" the banker asks.

"Dude, I'm going gambling. Throwing bones."

So tell me, how fast is that guy going to get kicked out of the bank?

You also can't walk into a bank and say, "I need to borrow fifteen hundred bucks because I've got to get a new apartment because my old lady caught me fooling around and kicked me out on the street."

Me? I don't care. If you've got something worth more than fifteen hundred bucks, I'll be glad to take it and give you the money. And if I'm lucky, you'll tell me the story of what happened between you and your old lady while I'm counting out the bills. Don't be surprised if I go ahead and ask.

If you walked into our back room, you'd be amazed that we can keep any of it straight. For one thing, the back of the shop is about four times bigger than the showroom. We're buying so much stuff and putting so much on pawn that it's hard to keep track. It's not air-conditioned, and on a 110-degree Vegas summer day, you could very easily mistake that back room for hell. That's why cleaning it has become such a joke on the show. If Old Man is mad at Chum, he'll tell him to go and clean the back room.

I don't think he's ever done it, but the threat works. As a joke, anyway.

PEOPLE WHO COME INTO the pawn shop use their material possessions the way people in the conventional world of finance and commerce use credit cards. And like someone using a credit card, they aren't usually looking to max out. They just want enough cash to get by. That piece of jewelry or table saw is their collateral to make it through a tough time.

I know popular culture has made it difficult for you to believe this, but I'll say it anyway: It's a good deal for them. Before you call me crazy, think about it.

You can come into my shop and get a loan. You can renege on the payment. You can get your stuff repossessed. But guess what? I'm *still* not going to turn you in to a credit agency. And I'm not going to sue you. Where else can you get that deal?

And the best part is, if you walk in the door a week later, I'll do business with you all over again. How's that for service?

It's nice to envision an ideal world, but we don't live in one. These are the facts of life, and I deal in the facts of life. Stuff happens and people need to be able to turn to someone. If we weren't there, most of these people would have to turn to friends or family—if they have one or the other or both—and how often does that turn out well? I'm not saying we're a house of philanthropy, but a pawn shop does serve a purpose to a certain segment of society that a lot of people would rather ignore.

Back before our industry became vilified, a slang term for pawnbroker used to be "Uncle." You'd think people who come in looking to pawn something would be ashamed or embarrassed, but the opposite is true. All of a sudden, their pawnbroker becomes their therapist. They'll tell me things they wouldn't tell their spouses or parents or siblings.

I'm the closest thing these people will ever have to a financial advisor. They ask my opinion on what they should do with their money, where they should look for work, whether their latest get-rich-quick scheme is as foolproof as they believe it is.

The interaction I have with our longtime customers is probably the best part of the job. There are people who have been doing business with us since my dad opened the buy-and-sell store on Fremont Street, almost thirty years ago. They are as much a part of the fabric of the store as my dad or Corey or Chumlee.

I have to be careful not to identify people here too precisely, or by name, because by law a pawn is a private transaction. I'm legally obligated not to reveal our customers' identities. In a strange consequence of the television show, that privacy law has kept my dad, Corey, Chumlee, and me from working the counter in the store any longer. With the crowds of people roaming the showroom, snapping photos and taking video of us, we can no longer feel comfortable with the confidentiality of the pawn transactions. When we're shooting the show, we close the shop temporarily and allow a handful of customers to stay in the showroom.

But there are certain people I tell the employees that I want to see whenever they come into the shop. Janie is an older Asian lady who started coming into the store when she was in her fifties, right after we opened. She's in her seventies now, and she still can't play enough slot machines. She's the sweetest lady, and if you saw her walking down the street you'd never imagine she's one of our most loyal customers. Or that she gambles the way the rest of us breathe.

Janie (not her real name, of course) comes into the store once a week, the same way she's been doing for more than twenty years. Literally once a week. She's either pawning something or picking something up. It runs in cycles; three or four weeks in a row she'll come in and pawn stuff so she can gamble, then she'll show up one day with an even bigger smile on her face, pay off her loans, and pick everything up at once.

Every time, without fail, she walks into the store and says, "Hey, Rick. How are the kids? How are you? How's everyone?"

People will be standing around the counter and she'll engage all of them.

"Oh, this Rick—he's the greatest person there is."

Everybody laughs, including me. (I might appreciate the sentiment, but even I think she's laying it on thick.) I don't know how Janie does it, but she's figured out a way to make this whole thing work for her. Pawning and picking up, pawning and picking up. She keeps all of it straight, and she always has a smile on her face.

THIS IS A CRAZY business. I can't say that often enough. I've met politicians, celebrities, athletes—every walk of life has walked through that door. The people-watching in the Gold & Silver Pawn Shop over the years has been top-notch. I'll put it up against any other place of business in the country.

For instance: The finance minister of a major Southeast Asian country was a semiregular customer. He came into the store six or seven times over the course of a few years. I can't name him or his country, but this guy was a major player—diplomatic passport and everything—who would show up in front of the store and climb out of the back of one of the casino limousines.

He always came in carrying bags of gold. Piles of it.

"I need to pawn," he said. "Casinos won't give me no credit."

The casinos wouldn't give him credit because there was no way for them to hold him accountable for his gambling debts. Once he left the country, they were out of luck. And the kind of money he gambled wasn't available at the nearest ATM. This guy needed serious cash.

And that's why the casinos, although they wouldn't give him credit, knew exactly where he could get some cash. Not only that, but they would personally drive him there—in style.

He didn't sell his gold because he always wanted to get it back. He'd pawn it, gamble to his heart's content, and then get money wired in to retrieve the gold. It was just the way he chose to do business.

On every visit after his first, he would bring us gifts. He was a gregarious, happy guy, but it was clear to us from the beginning why he insisted on pawning his gold instead of selling it: It wasn't his to sell. He was gambling with his country's money.

Oh, well—we aren't here to judge.

IF MEDICAL RESEARCHERS WANT to attempt to find the gambling gene, I've got the perfect family for them to study. These people—and again, it's important that I be somewhat vague—were phenomenally thorough in their compulsion to gamble.

The father owned several large antique shops in another state. When he died, the wife moved with her three sons—all in their thirties—to Las Vegas. They closed the stores and kept the merchandise.

All they did was gamble. All day every day, gamble gamble gamble.

We were their bank. One of the sons was the "banker" in their gambling enterprise, and he came into the store so frequently he should have had his own key. He'd pawn and pick up, pawn and pick up. One day I looked at him and said, "How in the world do you keep track of all this?"

He shrugged and said, "Oh, it's not that hard. We have a pretty good system."

They had been doing business with us for about eighteen months when curiosity got the best of me. I logged onto the computer to add up their pawns and pickups.

It takes a lot to astound me, but I was astounded.

Over the course of a year and a half, they'd had thirteen hundred pawns and thirteen hundred pickups. *Thirteen hundred!* A lot of times it was the same stuff going in and out, probably a couple of hundred items total, but still—this floored me. How could they possibly do that?

They didn't lose one thing. Not one! They got every single item back. This was like a streak that'll never be broken, like Joe DiMaggio's fifty-six-game hitting streak. That takes planning and organization, two things not normally associated with compulsive gamblers.

This family was an endless source of fascination for me. They had some money, and they apparently had the inventory from the businesses, but they simply wanted to live in a completely different way. These people were the embodiment of why I love what I do: unique people you'd never meet anywhere else in the world but Vegas, and nowhere else in Vegas but my shop.

The mother was a prim, nice-looking older woman, always dressed well. She looked like she spent quite a bit of time every morning putting herself together before she went out to the casino or the pawn shop. The sons were polite, clean, articulate guys. We always had good conversations. Apparently gambling didn't seem to tear the family apart. To the contrary, they were always together and always getting along. They didn't act as if their chosen lifestyle was any different than anybody else's. They enjoyed gambling, so they gambled.

They always gambled at one particular casino. There are perks, of course, to being a frequent guest, and this casino handed out raffle coupons every time a customer won a jackpot at a slot machine. The raffle was for a new house.

And I'll be goddamned if they didn't win the raffle! They were given the option of taking the house or $150,000 in cash.

They should have taken the house.

They chose the cash.

Which meant we went quite a while without seeing them. There was no need to pawn the antiques with that much money at their disposal.

And then, six months later, one of the brothers walked in with one of the antique pieces. They had gambled away the one hundred and fifty grand, and they were back to Gold & Silver Pawn to fund their enterprise the old-fashioned way.

When he came in, he wasn't sheepish or embarrassed. He matter-of-factly shook my hand and we discussed what had happened. I couldn't believe it. I knew they had won the money, but when he told me it was all gone I couldn't help myself.

"Are you fucking nuts?" I asked him, as politely as possible.

He kind of laughed a little, and for the first time I could see the faintest sign of embarrassment.

"If I were you guys, I would move as far away from this town as I could," I said. "I wouldn't want to see another casino again in my life."

He shrugged as if to say, *That's life.*

I shook my head and stared at him, slack-jawed. He really didn't have anything to say, and he didn't get pissed off at me for being so blunt. He knew how the system worked, and the family had made its decision: This is how they chose to live.

I wrote up his pawn slip, and things were back to normal for them. Pawn, pick up, pawn, pick up.

It was like the raffle never happened.

IT'S HARD TO BELIEVE in our age of big-box stores, of Wal-Marts and Costcos and Targets, but it wasn't all that long ago that our economy had room for specialty stores. There were stores that sold only shoes, and only dresses, and only suits. One of the more successful specialty-store chains sold only hosiery.

This one particular chain was huge, with fifteen hundred stores across the country. The owner of the chain also owned a significant piece of a major cosmetics company. The owner had children, and one of his sons turned out to be the black sheep, slightly wild and incorrigible and not fit for the polite society that swirls around folks who own hosiery empires.

He was nice to me, though. I liked him well enough. He was one of my customers for the better part of a decade. He might have been the family's outcast, but he wasn't aced out of the will. He lived in Vegas on a trust that paid him twenty-seven grand a month.

It wasn't close to enough.

He got paid at the beginning of every month, and by the fifteenth of every month, he was in the shop pawning all his shit. Like clockwork.

I was his de facto therapist. He'd come in with this sheepish look on his face and say, "Rick, I just can't live on twenty-seven grand a month."

"Well," I'd say, "I know a lot of people who'd like to try."

He'd laugh a little, but he really did believe that he couldn't live on that amount of money. He gambled not for sport or entertainment or the rush. It was like he gambled for sustenance, day and night, day after day, week after week. I'm sure he had to win some of the time, but it never seemed like it changed his routine. That trust was the only thing standing between him and a cardboard box on the street.

He was another guy you'd never guess was a degenerate gambler if you saw him walking around. He always wore a suit when he came into the shop, and he didn't appear to have any other vices. He wasn't a druggie, or a drinker, just a compulsive gambler. He talked about having a daughter in medical school, so maybe he had some other expenses that ate into his twenty-seven grand a month, but not enough to explain his continued presence at the pawn shop.

He used to crack me up because he'd come in and start bragging like a little kid about things that seemed insignificant to me. He liked to gamble at the Flamingo, and one day he walked in with a big smile on his face.

"You look happy today," I said.

"I am," he said. "Last night the Flamingo gave me my own parking spot."

He didn't look at this situation the way most of us would. I'm looking at him thinking, *If I owned a casino where you dropped more than twenty grand every month, I'd have no problem giving you a parking spot. I might even roll a red carpet up to the parking spot and make sure a hot babe met you at the door every time you put it in park.*

Him? No. He was just happy to have a special spot to park his car. Simple pleasures, I guess. It never occurred to him that he could rent an entire parking lot with the money he was losing on gambling.

Like most of my stories, this guy's story gets better. He had been telling me for a few years that he couldn't wait for his fiftieth birthday. Most people dread it, but he was looking forward to it because on that day he got a $3 million payout bonus from his trust fund.

His birthday came and he got his money.

It took him thirty-six hours to blow it at the Horseshoe.

He played craps and blackjack and whatever else.

Thirty-six hours to blow three million bucks.

I shit you not.

He walked back into the shop, holding something to pawn. I looked at him and my jaw dropped. "No," I said. "No. Don't tell me . . ."

He kind of made this sad face and shook his head and shrugged his shoulders.

As he was telling me the story, I thought I was going to be sick. *Thirty-six hours?* I thought. *You couldn't stop?* I didn't say anything, though, except to tell him I was sorry.

When he finished, there was a dead pause between us, but then he broke into a big smile.

"You know the good part?" he asked. "When I left, they guaranteed me a room for life at the Horseshoe."

THERE ARE SO MANY subcultures in our society. Races, religions, sexual orientations, occupations—representatives of all of them shop at the store. And I have learned something from each of them.

Up until our son Jake was born in 2003, my wife Tracy worked in the store. She was a great employee. Her manner exudes calm, which is a great advantage in a place that often feels like it's moving a million miles an hour. She was really good at helping people pick out jewelry, and she was remarkably patient with the customers. The old ladies loved her, that's for sure.

Another person who loved her was a transvestite who started coming in and looking at the jewelry. He was about five-foot-six, always needed a shave, and made a habit of wearing the shabbiest women's clothes you could find. There's nothing like a cross-dresser who has let himself go. He was quite a spectacle.

A lot of the men in the store—especially my dad, if you can believe that—didn't want anything to do with this guy. This was back when we had only twelve employees, so the available pool of salespeople was quite a bit smaller than it is now. This guy would walk in and clear out the counter. He might as well have been waving around an Uzi. Two steps inside the door and there'd be nobody there.

Tracy saw this happen a couple of times, and she felt bad for the guy. She also thought we were being ridiculous and childish by avoiding him, and she was right about that, too. Anyway, she has a different attitude. She looked at him and said, "He's fucking harmless. I'll help him."

She was extremely nice to him, and he liked that. I don't think he was used to being treated that way, so he really appreciated Tracy. Pretty soon he was spreading the word among the transvestite community in Vegas. *Go see this lady named Tracy. She'll take care of you.* It didn't take long before every transvestite in town was walking into the shop, looking around to get his bearings, and then asking, "Do you know where I can find Tracy?"

It got to the point where we'd just call Tracy out when one of them walked in. "Tracy, customer here for you." She knew what that meant, and the transvestites were happy when they didn't have to come up to one of us and ask.

Tracy had no problem with any of them, and they all bought jewelry. She had her own little subculture as her clientele. And the best part about transvestites is that they buy *big* jewelry. I don't know if they were overcompensating or what, but they bought the biggest, gaudiest jewelry we had in the store, and they bought a lot of it.

It turned out they were good for business, but when Tracy left, they took their business somewhere else. She told them, "I'm going to stay home and raise my son," but that didn't matter to them. They were upset, and they didn't come back.

I tell everyone that works for me: Don't look down on people. If you're nice to people, if you take a minute to talk to them, it's good for business whether they buy anything or not. Just because they don't look like they have money doesn't mean they don't have money.

You can't tell by looking at somebody, especially in this town, and especially in this business.

I learned that lesson shortly after I started in the business. We were struggling to make it through every day, and one day I got impatient while waiting on this little Asian lady. She looked like she didn't have a dime to her name. Her clothes were torn and she didn't look like she took care of herself. She was like a bag lady who didn't stink. She was asking me to pull out this piece of expensive jewelry and that piece of expensive jewelry, and the whole time I'm thinking this is an absolute waste of my time.

About the time I was ready to walk away and tell her I didn't have time to do this all day long, she pointed to one of the most expensive pieces and said, "I'll take that one."

I'm stunned. I'm thinking, *There's no possible way.*

She reached down and pulled four grand out of her sock.

Out of her fucking *sock.*

With my mouth hanging open, I took the piece out and walked it over to the register.

That's the last time I let my assumptions affect the way I treated a customer.

I HAVE A PAIR of alligator cowboy boots in the back room that a guy literally took off his feet to sell to me.

He walked up to me, pointed to his boots, and said, "Twenty bucks?"

I looked them over and said, "Sure."

He kicked them off right there in the shop, took a twenty-dollar bill, and walked out of the shop in his socks.

When I tell that story, people always get this disgusted look on their faces. They scrunch up their noses and ask, "And you *took* them?"

I answer, "Hell, yes I did—they were my size."

Really, it's just stuff. I can't emphasize that enough. I don't have a personal connection to it. Sure, I love a lot of the cool things we have in the shop. I love some of it so much I won't sell it. But I always cringe when people ask, "Don't you think it's morally wrong to buy stuff that has sentimental value to them?"

No. Just no. Again, it's *stuff.* A roof over your head or an education for your kids is more important than a little Tiffany box that was handed down from your great-grandmother.

Here's a perfect example of how I view material possessions: I've gone through about twenty wedding rings. Most of them I've sold right off my finger. I don't have one right now, but the last one I had was platinum. I sold a lady's wedding ring in the store that was made out of platinum. My jeweler came to me and said, "We don't have any platinum sizing stuff."

I took my ring off and said, "Now you do." What was I going to do? I was getting $11,000 for the lady's ring.

Everybody falls in love with what they have, but sometimes what they think they have isn't what they really have. I've had people come in thinking they have the perfect diamond because their grandfather bought it for their grandmother and everybody in the family always said it was a perfect diamond because Grandpa said it was.

I have to be the one to break it to them: Grandpa was cheap.

As you've seen on the television show countless times, there are a lot of fakes out there. A guy walked in one summer afternoon with his wife. He was wearing a Red Sox cap and a Red Sox T-shirt, and he was interested in selling his Red Sox 2007 World Series ring. He was a member of the organization in some behind-the-scenes capacity—bat boy or clubhouse guy—and he wanted to know how much he could get for his ring.

Everything about the ring checked out, but when I took out my jeweler's magnifier—known as a loupe—and looked closely at the inside, I could see the Josten's brand mark was not consistent with every other

Josten's mark I've ever seen. It was a hand-carved J and not the typical emblem.

I showed it to the guy and explained what it was supposed to look like, but he was convinced I was wrong. He was cool about it, but his wife was starting to get agitated about one of two possibilities: (1) someone gave her husband an illegitimate World Series ring; or (2) her husband never had a real World Series ring.

I felt bad for the guy, and someone might wonder whether anyone who came into the store would know enough to check the emblem. The answer is yes. People who are serious collectors—which means those who would consider spending more than twenty grand on a World Series ring—would make it their business to know the difference. And that's why I don't deal in someone else's sentiment.

Look, you're dealing with a guy who buys gold teeth all the time. I'm the only pawn shop in town that'll do that. Old people know the deal; they know the teeth are worth money. They're the ones who come in to sell them after making sure their dentist gives the tooth to them after it's been pulled.

All of the young people who work in the shop will look at the teeth and say, "*Ewww.*"

You know what I tell them? "Take the damn thing. You can wash your hands afterward."

Everybody sees the equation from my side, but they never flip it over and look at it from the other end. Take the example of the guy with the alligator boots: If he hadn't had them, there's a good chance he wouldn't have eaten that day.

THE BEST NIGHTS IN Vegas are fight nights. Big fight nights. Those nights are Vegas at its best: teeming masses of humanity flowing down the sidewalks like water; people hanging out of the windows of honking cars; degenerate gamblers throwing bones shoulder to shoulder with A-list celebrities.

Anything's possible on a fight night.

The best fight nights were always the Mike Tyson fight nights, because he brought out an amazing array of humanity. The night Tupac Shakur was murdered on the street was a Tyson fight night. (Against Bruce Seldon, for you trivia buffs.) The night they closed the tables at the MGM Grand amid the stampeding frenzy of gunfire in the lobby (reported, never proved) was the night Tyson chomped on Evander Holyfield's ear.

If you wanted to know what America looks like when it's off the rails, when it's letting its hair down and not giving a shit, you needed to spend a night in Vegas on a Mike Tyson fight night.

And if you happened to be working the night window at Gold & Silver Pawn on a fight night, you never had a second to yourself. You got to see the drifters, the leftovers, the people who spilled down Las Vegas Boulevard, away from the glitz and glamour and bright lights. People would be frenzied down here, too, like the sidewalks were electrified. It was unlike anything else.

The rise and fall of Tyson seemed like a uniquely Vegas story. He moved here permanently shortly after he won the heavyweight title, and all his outlandish stories seemed to take place here. He bought a ridiculously huge estate, married Robin Givens, had tigers and cheetahs and whatever other exotic animals as pets—he was an outsized Vegas story in every respect.

Everything about Tyson was big news around here. When it started coming out that he was essentially bankrupt, a gang of five landscape guys came into the shop. They were down and out, and they were carrying all their tools to pawn.

About two weeks later, they came marching in together, laughing and joking. They were as happy this time as they were sad the last time. They paid to get their stuff back, and one of them said, "Now it's time to go shopping."

I said, "I've got to ask: You guys win the lottery or something?"

They laughed at that, and one of them said, "No, but close. We just got crazy money for repossessing all of Mike Tyson's palm trees."

It turned out a nursery had hired them to go to Tyson's house and pull all of these enormous palm trees out of the ground, load them up, and bring them back. They were getting a few hundred dollars per tree.

That, to me, is a quintessential Vegas story.

One man's misfortune is another man's fortune.

My dad, twenty-one
years old, in a 1962
Navy photo.

Family portrait, 1968:
My mom Joanne and
Old Man in the back.
I'm on the right,
about four years old,
with my brothers
Chris (middle) and
Joe (left).

Mom and Dad on a trip to Vegas in the early 1970s.

Here I am, full of energy and bad thoughts, in fifth grade.

Here I am at twenty-two, with a full head of hair in the shop at 413 Fremont Street.

My two oldest sons, circa 1997: Corey (right) is four years old, Adam is three.

The original shop, three hundred square feet at 1501 Las Vegas Blvd. South. Gold & Silver was the first shop in Vegas to buy and sell gold twenty-four hours a day. This building, which housed our business for six years, is eight blocks from our current location.

This 1950s Coke machine, bought for $3,500 and on sale for $4,995, was one of the first to allow purchasers to buy more than one flavor of soda. Before this machine, one flavor: Coke.

This ormolu clock, from the early 1800s, had to have been made by someone under thirty-five years old, since almost all gilders who worked with mercury to produce these clocks died by that age. I coined the term "Death Clock" for these; it helps sales. This one, on sale for $9,500, was purchased for $5,000.

The piece on the right is a three-hundred-year-old thunder mug, also known as a signal cannon. Used on ships, it was fired off to announce arrival in port. When port officials heard the cannon, they came out to board the ships to check for disease or contraband, and to collect taxes. The piece on the left is an 1800s explosive projectile—minus the explosives—used in cannons until after the Civil War. Both pieces are roughly three inches in diameter across the bottom.

This 1920s Gibson ukulele/ banjo is a bizarre instrument that nobody knows how to play. It is unique because its drumhead is original and has more than two hundred signatures from the 1920s from random people.

plans for the World War II attack on Iwo Jima were sold to me by a man looking to finance his daughter's wedding. Since then, I have done extensive research and can find no others. I vowed not to sell either of these, but I sold one for $10,000. I'm keeping the other one.

American long jumper Joe Greene's bronze medals from the 1992 Olympic Games in Barcelona and the 1996 Games in Atlanta. Each of the Olympic medals—gold, silver, and bronze—carry identical markings with the likeness of the goddess Nike.

This is a Blunderbuss-style musket made by a famous Italian maker named Lazarino in the 1650s. Lazarino's work was so good and his guns so popular that people were faking them as early as the late 1650s. This one has the original barrel but was restocked in the early 1700s.

Both of these Super Bowl rings came from players who rarely saw the field. The Patriots' first Super Bowl ring (right) is extremely valuable because owner Bob Kraft ignored NFL rules regarding ring size and the number of diamonds to produce a truly gaudy piece of jewelry. The two horses on the Broncos' ring denote the team's second Super Bowl victory. The Broncos' player traded the ring to his landlord for six months' worth of rent, and I bought it off the landlord.

The top sword is my samurai sword that has been dated back to 1490. It presents one of the most vexing issues of my career: There is a chip in the blade that will cost $6,000 to $8,000 to repair, but the act of repairing the chip could crack the blade and render it worthless.

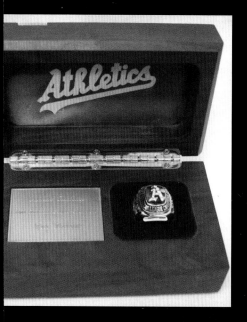

Known affectionately by me as a "Loser's Ring," this Oakland Athletics American League Championship ring was sold to me by a staff member. Even staff members' rings are valuable; I'm asking $11,000.

A Fire-Chief gas pump is cool Americana, and people love to buy them for their game rooms. I try to get one or two a year. This one is from the late 1940s or early 1950s, and here's an interesting fact: Its highest setting is 35.9 cents per gallon.

This Remington pearl-handled revolver is a cute little girl gun that shoots .22 caliber bullets and dates back to the 1870s. It was manufactured for a lady to carry in her purse.

This small, .22 caliber Derringer double-barreled revolver dates back to the 1860s or 1870s. Because of their age, people automatically believe they are worth a lot of money, but they weren't expensive when they were made and they still aren't. They made a ton of them, and since people don't throw away guns, there are a ton of them still on the market. This one's yours for $100.

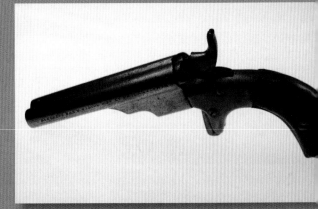

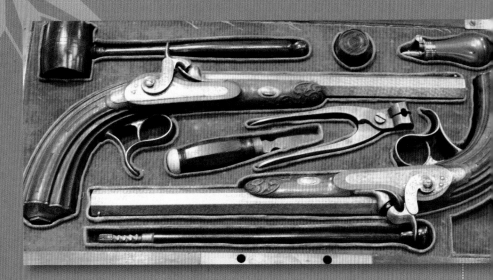

This is a rare item that also happens to be incredibly cool: a target pistol kit from the 1830s. This kit contains everything you could possibly need for these pistols. It was a rich man's toy, found by a construction worker in an attic. I'm asking $9,800.

OLD MAN

IF THERE'S ONE LESSON I'VE TAUGHT MY son Rick and my grandson Corey, it's the importance of taking sentiment out of business. You can probably gather from watching the television show that I'm not a sentimental guy when it comes to people's stuff, but I'm going to tell you straight-out anyway.

If a guy comes marching into the shop spouting about sentimental value, I've got no time for it. "Oh, this means so much to me and my family." Really? Then go home and put it in a goddamn drawer. 'Cuz that's where it belongs. And 'cuz I ain't paying for your sentimental value.

Besides, it's not my sentiment; it's yours. To me, it's just something I have to store and then sell. I love the rare and unusual stuff that comes through the door, but I only like it if it's something I can make a buck from. If it ain't, then it doesn't mean anything to me. I'm worried about two things: The price I pay and the price I sell. I'm pretty black-and-white that way.

There's a phrase I heard a long time ago and adopted as my own: *All gold is not yellow.* I think it fits my philosophy: If I can make money off something, I'm going to buy it. I can sell anything. I could walk out of my office right now and sell every single thing in the case. I might not get the price I want for it, but I could sell it. No doubt in my mind.

I tell my employees, "Use common sense." There are a lot of things I want to buy, but I'll let stuff walk if I can't get it at the price I want. And I know one thing: There's always going to be something walking in behind it. It's a lot like poker, and I know about poker, too. I supported myself in the navy playing poker, and blackjack, and loaning out money on account of me being the paymaster. I've been playin' poker one way or another every day since.

I'll tell you something else: Being a television personality makes it a lot harder for me to get my work done. Before we had the television show, we had twelve employees. Now we have forty-seven. We've got an entire crew of people who do nothing but sell T-shirts and bobbleheads and other kinds of crazy stuff.

A lot of it's crazy stuff with Chumlee's face plastered all over it. I see enough of that guy to know I don't want to be walking around with his face on my T-shirt. Or shot glass. Or baseball cap. Or whatever else they can think of to put his face on.

We've had to turn the daily operation of the shop over to people outside the family because we're so involved in filming and promoting the show. We've got departments for this, and departments for that. It ain't what it used to be. I still come to work every day, though, no later than 7:30 A.M., and I try to keep track of everything that comes in the shop and everything that goes out.

Back in the day, I could tell you to within a hundred dollars how much cash we had in the safe at any given time. I could tell you within a couple hundred dollars how much business we'd done at any given time during the day.

When we had a handful of employees, the shop was truly a family business. Now that we're bigger, we're still trying to run it like a family. It's just a damned large family now. We're doing the kind of volume that you'd associate with a big corporation, but we're trying not to lose the sense of family. I guess every successful business goes through growing pains. I still check on my employees and make sure they're being treated properly. We're one of the few businesses that provides full medical benefits to every employee and their families, and they don't pay a dime for it.

I don't have to work anymore. The day I walk in here and it's not fun, I won't walk back in the place. But damn, I love it in here. It's new every minute. Something different every time you turn around. This type of energy is hard to find anywhere else.

But it's changed. I can't deny that. On a typical day now, I get to the shop in the morning, have some coffee, and take a look at the receipts from the night crew. I make sure we open on time. I check the line outside to make sure the security people are doing their jobs. That's another by-product of the television show: We've had to hire someone to stand outside to keep order and let people in sixty at a time. Some mornings there are a hundred people out there waiting for us to open the door.

I can't work the counter anymore. I can't, Rick can't, Corey can't, Chumlee can't. Not that I want Chumlee working the counter, but he can't anyway. I can't tell you the name of someone who walked in here and pawned something, even if it was Barack Obama or Tom Cruise. It's against the law. So if I'm standing at the counter writing up a ticket for a pawn, there are fifty people crowded around taking pictures and videos. It kind of takes the "private" out of "private transaction," so we have to stay in the back of the store unless we're filming or someone comes in with something unusual we have to take a look at.

The only time we come out is to pose for pictures. It sure is nice that people like us enough to go out of their way to come into the shop and get their picture taken with an old man like me, but we can't stand there all day long. Sometimes people get irritated when I tell 'em I've got to go back and do some work.

So that's what success has caused: I can't even work in my own shop. Ain't that the damnedest thing?

I TELL PEOPLE I'VE got one of the most dysfunctional families in the world, but I do my best to hold it together. I think I do a good job of that. It might not always be pretty, but we make it work.

Here's something you should probably know about Rick as a kid: He was a fucking handful. That's the only way I can accurately put it. They all were, but he was the worst.

You want an example? I'll tell you a story: When Rick was a teenager, we took a family trip to Hawaii. I was in the navy, so we stayed in a military hotel on Oahu. I was feeling generous and we were on vacation, so I gave each of the three boys twenty bucks a day to buy some food and whatever else.

As far as I could tell, the vacation went well. The kids stayed out of our hair and had their fun. I didn't hear any complaining.

On the morning we were flying back to San Diego, I checked out of the hotel and got hit with a six-hundred-dollar restaurant and room service bill. That's when I learned Rick was ordering from room service and eating from the restaurant and charging everything to the room. He was eating goddamn lobster on my dime.

What a horrible little kid he was.

The biggest problem I've had with Rick over the years is simple: He's smarter than me, and he knows it. Now, don't get the wrong idea: I'm pretty damn smart myself. But that kid was always a step ahead of everybody, whether it was teaching himself to build his own house or becoming an expert in old coins or figuring out how to put a lobster dinner on my hotel tab. He's book smart and street smart. That's a tough combination for any dad.

* * * *

I WENT INTO THE navy in October 1958 and got out for the first time in February 1962. I stayed out for fourteen months, and I went back into the navy to get medical benefits for my daughter Sherry.

JoAnne and I have been married for fifty-one years, and there have been some ups and downs along the way. We've had our share of heartbreak. Little Sherry was born disabled, with Down syndrome. She was the light of my life for the short time we had her. She was six when she passed away, and there's a little bit of her still alive in all of our hearts. I believe that.

I loved the navy. It kept me away from home a lot, though. I was on ships for most of the 1960s and '70s, and by the time the three boys—Joe, Rick, and Chris—became teenagers it became too hard for JoAnne to handle. I had been in about twenty years by that time, and I would have stayed in for thirty, but three teenagers changed those plans.

I told my wife when I came home that I'd never leave her again, and I haven't. Except for going to work, we've been together ever since. That's one of the reasons I don't go on all the publicity tours for the show; she's in pretty poor health, and it's too hard for her to travel. She tells me to go anyway, but I didn't until Chumlee and I went on a trip to Indiana to do a personal appearance at an Indian casino. The people there seemed like they couldn't get enough of us. But other than that, I go to the shop and head home to JoAnne. It's all about demographics and I don't fit the demographic. That's fine with me; I'd rather stay home and work anyway.

It's funny to me that we're so closely associated with Las Vegas, because I had no idea I'd ever end up here. My wife opened her real estate office in San Diego in 1973. She ran it, and I worked part-time there. It went along pretty well until 1981, when interest rates got up to 18 percent and we damned near went completely bankrupt.

I had to do something. We didn't have much, and I'd always bought and sold gold on the side for a little extra cash. The real estate market didn't have any appeal to us anymore, and we weren't about to sit around and wait for it to recover.

I got the idea to move to Las Vegas and open a store where I could sell gold and silver, maybe get to the point where I could open a pawn shop someday. Why not Vegas, right? It's got to be the best place to be a hustler, and at that point hustling's about all I had going for me.

We moved out here in April of 1981 with about $5,000 to our name. I opened my little buy-and-sell store in a three-hundred-square-foot shop at 1501 South Las Vegas Boulevard. Called it Gold & Silver Coin Shop. Five years later we moved from that spot to Fremont Street, near the huge downtown parking garage, and in 1987 we got our license as a secondhand store.

We lost our lease there and eventually landed where we are now in 1988. It hasn't been easy, I'll tell you that, and if Rick hadn't been so goddamned persistent about getting us a pawn license in 1989 I don't know where we'd be right now. Can you believe Rick called the city statistician every single week? That's the kind of persistence I admire. It's a family trait.

People want to know the secret to success. Here's mine: I worked seven days a week, ten hours a day, for ten years with no vacation. That ain't a secret, that's just life. I had to do that to make this place work. I was so damned stubborn I wouldn't quit. I didn't know how it was gonna work, and I didn't know *if* it was gonna work. I just knew I had to be here to make it work. It wasn't gonna happen all by itself.

THERE ARE MOMENTS THAT can change your life as a businessman. Sometimes it's luck, sometimes it's hard work, sometimes the two come together. Getting a television show is one moment. Another one happened to me before we got our pawn license, when we were running the little gold and silver shop in the early 1980s on Las Vegas Boulevard South.

A fella by the name of Al Benedict was president of the MGM Grand. At the time, the MGM was probably the biggest and best-known casino/hotel in Vegas. Well, one night Al was robbed of close to a hundred grand in jewelry, and the Vegas cops made it known it was a priority to find whoever did it and make him pay.

Within hours of the robbery they distributed photos of the jewelry along with an artist's sketch of the suspect. They knew the robber might end up at a pawn shop or a secondhand store or a hole-in-the-wall, three-hundred-square-foot buy-and-sell store like ours. It was a good bet this guy wasn't stealing a hundred grand worth of jewelry because he liked the design. We taped the flyers to the back of the counter, where we could see them but the customers couldn't.

Sure enough, a couple of days later a guy comes waltzing in with some jewelry. He fits the composite sketch, and the jewelry matches up, too. I talked to him for a little bit and tried to distract him while I grabbed a shotgun out from underneath the counter. I held that shotgun down around my knees so he couldn't see it until I came around the corner. By then, it was too late for the poor son of a bitch.

I was probably a little quicker on my feet back then, and when I got around the corner, I pointed the shotgun at his chest and told him to hit the goddamned floor or bits of him would be all over the shop. I stood over him with the shotgun until the cops got there. Damned guy got more than he bargained for, if you ask me. By the look on his face, I don't think he expected that kind of reception.

The Vegas police showed up and cuffed him. Shook my hand, too. I made them look good, and from that point forward we were treated right by the police. We helped them, and they helped us. To this day, if we hit the alarm in the shop, they're here within seconds.

Al Benedict was happy about it, too. I was a VIP in the MGM for as long as he was in charge. He told all his employees to treat me right, and I couldn't even leave a tip in that building for a long, long time.

It didn't stop there. They sent business our way, too. The rich Japanese gamblers who couldn't get markers? MGM sent 'em to us with their Rolexes and Patek Philippes. They sent their winners to us, too—people who had taken the MGM's money and maybe wanted to buy a Rolex or Patek Philippe. It worked for both sides.

But the way I look at it, that bastard with the stolen jewelry was trying to screw me over, too. I wasn't going to sit back and let him rob me by selling the shop something hot. But the whole Rambo deal with the shotgun wasn't a big deal. It wasn't the first time I stuck a shotgun in someone's face to protect my business interests.

Who knows? It might not be the last, either.

I LOVE CRAZES. THAT'S something I taught Rick, and he taught Corey. It's the lifeblood of this business. I love it when people get excited over something like a Tickle Me Elmo doll and we can make money off their craziness. People go wild over stuff and they're willing to pay anything to get their hands on something they think might be worth more down the line.

And then, just as fast, these crazes end. You don't know when they're going to start, and you don't know when they're going to end. Your only hope is that you can get into that wave at the right time and ride it as long as it lasts.

Like Rick says, if you have a sociology degree, you'd throw it away if you spent a day watching the people in the shop. You can learn more about human nature here than in any classroom.

Here's a short list of things that made us serious money: blue jeans,

Zippo lighters, bomber jackets, Tickle Me Elmo dolls, baseball cards, comic books.

Bomber jackets. Oh, I *loved* bomber jackets.

Back in the day—when we were just a gold and silver shop—a guy came in with a ton of stuff to sell. People knew I would buy things and then look to sell them at flea markets and swap meets. He had model trains and dolls and comic books and a hundred other things. Deep in the pile of stuff were two World War II bomber jackets.

That weekend we gave the bomber jackets to a good friend who was setting up a booth at a flea market. He put those two bomber jackets on the counter, and within minutes a couple of Japanese guys walked up and tried them on.

"How much for these jackets?" one of them asks.

"Seven each," our friend says.

They don't blink an eye. They nod their heads and reach into their pockets, where they pull out a roll of hundreds and peel off seven *thousand* each for the bomber jackets.

Our friend was thinking seven *hundred*, but he didn't argue.

That's when we knew bomber jackets were going to be another irrational craze.

And that's when Rick started doing whatever he could, just short of breaking his neck, to get his hands on bomber jackets.

ONE THING YOU'VE GOT to do in this business: Be careful who you hire. We've lost half a million dollars to employee theft over the years. We deal so much in cash, the temptation is great. And if the economy's bad for the people coming into the store, it's probably bad for the people looking for a job in the store. We've got to be careful, because some people are looking for the easy way out.

I've got one guy who sits all day long looking at the cameras. The cameras are on the employees. That's his job—to sit there and watch the employees.

Right now, as I sit here, we've got more than a million dollars out in loans. I have $290,000 worth of stuff sitting in the back room that we paid out in pawns over the last thirty days. It's a bookkeeping nightmare: We're buying stuff every day, stuff comes off pawn every day. But I'll tell you what: We balance the cash every day to within two or three dollars.

We pay our people good. I've had other pawnbrokers chew me out because I pay my people too much. We give them full medical. We give them bonuses. We try to treat them well.

It used to cost me five thousand a day in overhead just to open that front door. Since we got a television show, it costs me ten thousand a day. More customers, more sales, more security, more employees. It's all good in the end. One thing that gets lost in the glitz and glamour of the television show: It's goddamned hard work to run a business like this and make it as successful as we have.

Now that people have seen the show, they want to know what we're like as people, how we interact as a family.

Rick and I have a good rapport. I respect him and he respects me.

He'll tell you he runs the store, I'll tell you I run it.

Together we've taken the pawn industry from a gray-area business to Middle America. The television show has legitimized our business. All the pawnbrokers love the show because we display it exactly how it is.

There is no college for creating pawnbrokers. You're going to make mistakes, and you're going to find yourself in the position where you're standing there with a dumb look on your face while you stare at something that you've never seen before. And you'll have no idea what the hell it is.

My answer is usually to buy the damn thing. I'm a pack rat. Rick and I have our differences about that sometimes. I always want more.

My role on the show is to be an old grump, and I guess that's pretty true. Nobody thought *Pawn Stars* was going to mushroom like it has. We didn't think so, History didn't think so. We thought we'd get a couple of years out of it and be happy. But Leftfield Pictures put together a great format, and it works. They've done a great job of transferring what we do to television.

Any family business creates jealousies, and if you add the money and attention you get from a television show, it's bound to be worse. So yes, we've got our jealousies in the family. Rick's older brother Joe is feeling it, and Rick's son Adam is a little envious of Corey's newfound fame. It's natural for people to feel that way, but this entire television experience feels like one big fluke. Rick always wanted a show—there were many times I thought he was crazy—but nobody can say we planned it out this way. Damned thing just happened.

There are a lot of older people who love the show, but they're more interested in getting the people from eighteen to fifty-four years old. They're the ones spending money. My wife can't understand why I'm not getting all the personal appearances that the other guys are getting. Rick and Corey and Chumlee are appearing at casinos and traveling around to trade shows to collect appearance fees. I understand it—it's demographics. Nothing surprising about that.

Besides, I had never watched a reality show until I was starring in one.

When people ask me what I think about all this attention, I tell them the same thing every time:

We'll ride this horse till it dies, and then we'll cut a steak off its ass.

IT'S JUST STUFF

**WORE A FAKE ROLEX ON MY WRIST FOR** five years to remind me that I'm not always as smart as I think I am. The fake was no one's fault but my own; I bought it, so I wore it.

One day fifteen years ago, a guy came in with the watch, and it seemed like a pretty straightforward transaction. I looked it over, it was a Rolex, and I gave him $5,000 for it. Even then, I considered myself to be something of an expert in fakes. I knew what I was doing, I knew what to look for, and I knew how to detect the slightest difference between the real thing and a facsimile. If I didn't, I would have been out of business.

Usually, I can look at something for a few seconds and point out ten different inconsistencies that indicate a fake. If you see enough of them, and I do, it becomes almost second nature. There are certain aspects of a watch—whether it's a Rolex or a Patek Philippe or one of the other high-enders—that are unique to the maker. They're little trademarks that separate the best watches from good watches, and those signature marks make life easier for people like me who have to be on the lookout for scammers trying to sell fakes.

You have to remember: There are people out there whose sole purpose in life—for fun and profit—is to go around trying to screw over pawn shops. They're out there, and guys like me have to look out for them.

But until the moment this particular watch came through the door, I was unaware just how far some people will go to produce a fake Rolex.

This watch had a 1970s Rolex movement, which means someone bought a beatup Rolex from the seventies for probably $700 or $800. They took the movement out of that watch and put a new dial on it, then new hands on it, then new crystal. All of these were legitimate Rolex parts, so on first glance there was no way of telling this was a phony watch.

But here's the crazy part: They *made* an eighteen-carat case and band. They did such a good job that it was difficult to tell the difference. I had checked out the internals first—they're usually the first place a fake is exposed. Since this one checked out internally, I got complacent and gave a cursory check to the rest of the watch. And that's how I completely missed out on the fake case and band.

By making such a refined fake, these guys weren't working with the same margins as someone who was trying to pawn off a $500 fake as real. The cheap fakes, if they're successful, can turn a 1,000 percent profit. The problem, of course, is finding someone who will be fooled enough to hand over $5,000. The smart guys can walk into our shop, look into our cases, and immediately realize we're not the kind of place that will be easily bamboozled by a cheap fake. (Although when Corey was working the night window his first few weeks on the job, it was a different story. Now, however, we'd like to think we've closed that loophole.)

A lot of fakes are easy to spot. Some are just versions of old scams. I still occasionally get people trying to pull the old "White Van Speaker Scam." This one is a classic, and it's been around so long I'm left to conclude it has worked on enough people to keep it going.

It works like this: Guys troll the streets, almost always in a white work van, looking for someone who looks like they can afford to buy some new in-home speakers. (Or a pawn shop, where they think we'll buy anything.) They get your attention and then proceed to give a grand performance, telling you how they've fallen into this sweet deal on speakers. They just finished an installation and they found they have speakers left over. These speakers sell for $4,000, but instead of giving them back, they're willing to sell them to you for just $400.

They have glossy brochures detailing all the features of the speakers. They sound and look legitimate. They have delivery invoices and business cards. It's a very organized scam—but it's a scam. The speakers are worth maybe $40 a pair.

The watch I wore as a reminder was by far the best fake I'd ever seen. And it didn't come cheap. By the time they were finished, they probably had put $2,500 to $3,000 into this watch, and I bought it for $5,000. It was smart for them—they came close to doubling their money—but it blew me away that someone would go to such extraordinary lengths to pull this off.

Wearing the watch had the desired effect. Every time I glanced at it, it screamed out at me: *You don't know everything!*

And besides, it was a decent watch to wear around.

You know, it was *sort* of a Rolex.

THE SEMI-FAKE ROLEX WAS also a reminder to me that I *can't* know everything. It's like the serenity prayer; you have to accept the things you cannot know. I might try to read and study as much as I can about a million different diverse topics, but certain things are simply impossible. Those things drive me crazy.

Take Confederate swords. There are so many fakes out there you can't truly tell the difference. Confederate swords are unique because they were of such poor quality from the beginning. It's like there never really were new or authentic Confederate swords.

There was next to zero manufacturing in the South. Confederate soldiers were carrying around Union swords that somehow found their way into their hands. The South also bought all kinds of weapons, including swords, from the English. These used swords, a lot of them broken and battered, would be sent over from England, and the Confederate soldiers were putting the CSA emblem on themselves. They would take a piece of metal, coat the back in wax, and push it onto the sword. From there, they would pour muriatic acid over the top, and it would etch the initials CSA onto the sword.

If this was a legitimate etching, done in 1861, it wouldn't look any different than an etching that was done a year ago. The age of the sword could be determined, but the emblem is another story. There's really no way of telling the difference. I can't tell you how much that annoys a guy like me.

One of my employees, the one we call "Shrek," came in one day with three signed documents, one each from George Washington, James Monroe, and Herbert Hoover. I'm sitting in the office with my dad, and Shrek says, "The guy says he wants thirteen thousand dollars for the three of them."

Old Man says, "That's nice of him. Tell him no. I ain't gonna pay no thirteen thousand dollars. I'll pay five."

That's a typical negotiation tactic from my dad. If I offer someone $3,000 for an item and they counter with $4,000, there's a good chance Old Man is going pipe in with $2,000. It's just who he is. In contrast to my dad, I go into a different kind of work mode. I get quiet and start looking at the signed papers to see what I think of them, if I can find any obvious problems that might indicate they're fakes.

Shrek says, "He says he wants to sell them, so he's going to leave his information—"

"Is he local?" I ask.

Old Man says, "Just go out there and buy 'em, Rick."

I'm still looking.

"Hold on a second," I tell my dad.

"The Monroe one is in pretty rough condition," Shrek says. "It looks like it got wet and the ink faded through onto the other side."

I'm still quiet. I honestly don't know how much time passes while this is happening. I don't really hear the conversation around me. I love these moments; it's like a puzzle to me.

I point to the Washington paper. "I'll give him five grand for that one," I say. "But I need to get someone in here to verify the signatures."

Then I turn to the Monroe document. I look at it for a few minutes and say, "I can almost one hundred percent guarantee you this is one hundred percent bullshit fake."

The ink was a modern ink. On the George Washington paper, the ink had turned brown. The coloring in old ink was black with iron filings. When it oxidizes, it turns brown. On the Monroe paper, the ink remained black. That made it suspect—the ink at that time wouldn't have retained its color.

My job is to be naturally skeptical. I can't assume that all three items are valid just because one is. I can't ever take something on face value, because that's when I'll get burned.

That's what some sellers don't understand. They can come in with a signed letter from a president that looks legitimate, and to a certain point it is. The age of the item checks out, the stationery checks out, but you have to know more than that. Presidents are busy people; very often letters and things that are less official are signed by secretaries. You know, "Here's a stack of letters. Sign them for the President."

Letters signed by secretaries are essentially worthless. And the other thing I have to deal with is a fundamental fact of business: The people who are going to come into my shop and be interested in buying an extremely expensive piece of history are savvy enough to know the difference between a secretary's signature and a president's signature. They wouldn't be serious collectors, with serious bank accounts, if they weren't. So what that means is a seller who is interested in getting some money for a very cool piece of memorabilia isn't seeing the world from the same vantage point I am.

I LIKE THE STORIES behind the items as much—if not more— than the items themselves. Walking around the shop, I look at this stuff as living history. It presents a narrative of a time, place, and people vastly different from how we live now. That's why the shop, to me, could be viewed as one of the most eclectic museums around.

There are great stories behind and under every piece of glass in the building, but my ormolu clocks are some of my favorites. I have three of them right now, and if you walked around the showroom you probably wouldn't pick them to be among the most fascinating and history-filled pieces in the shop. They're about eighteen inches tall and a foot wide, but the story they tell is far bigger.

Ormolu means "crushed gold" in French, and these clocks were made in the early 1800s throughout France by mercury gilders whose patience and precision would be difficult to duplicate in our modern world.

And there's this fact, too: These clockmakers died for their work.

They started with a brass body, which was then soaked in mercury nitrate—a mercury and nitric acid mixture. The nitric acid etched the brass and allowed the mercury to adhere to the body of the clock. At this point, it looked silver, like mercury. Alchemists discovered hundreds of years ago, probably before the Roman Empire, that gold and silver would be sucked into mercury, and the next step in the process called for the clockmakers to take gold amalgam (crushed gold mixed with mercury) and dab it onto the body of the clock.

They would dab this mixture, which had the consistency of a liquidy paste, onto the clock for days and days. Eventually, the gold started transferring onto the clock. After this painstaking process, there were probably five or six grams of gold attached to the clock.

Handling this amount of mercury with no safeguards—no gloves, masks, nothing—seems suicidal on its own. However, this wasn't the worst these guys had to endure. After the dabbing step was done, they put the clock—or whatever they were gilding—into an oven to burn off the mercury and create the brilliant gold finish that is the hallmark of the ormolu clock.

These gilders breathed those mercury fumes until the mercury was completely removed from the clock. Mercury poisoning is about the worst thing you can imagine. It's a hideous death.

The gilders rarely lived to be forty years old. Most of them lost their minds far sooner. They didn't know any better, but it's sobering to wonder how many of these guys died before someone made the connection between their deaths and their occupation.

Mercury gilding was outlawed by the 1850s, so these clocks will never be duplicated. Thankfully. I call these clocks "Ormolu Death Clocks" because of the story behind them. They're roughly $15,000 apiece, and they also sell a lot better with a tag that calls them death clocks.

For one thing, it makes anyone who is interested ask why the clocks are called that.

And for another, I get to tell them a story.

I'VE GOT SOME OTHER favorites, too. One of the most iconic pieces we have in the shop is a painting of Jim Morrison by Denny Dent. You see it behind the counter on nearly every show. It's one of the first things people recognize when they walk into the shop, and it's one of the most photographed. I have two Denny Dents in the shop: Morrison and Bob Marley.

Dent is a fascinating story. He worked in a Carlos Murphy's in Lake Tahoe and painted live in the restaurant. He was a speed painter—he painted portraits in less than five minutes and got paid $50 a night by the restaurant and whatever he could get for his paintings. He painted on a roll of construction paper, and he just painted as many portraits as he could in a night. He'd take $10 or $20 for a painting, or he'd just paint in exchange for his bar bill.

Most of his Carlos Murphy's paintings were thrown away as soon as the people got home. Nobody knew this guy who was painting for a bar bill in a Mexican-Irish chain restaurant was going to end up being anything more than a novelty act, like a guy walking around twisting balloons into animal shapes.

Celebrities were Dent's passion. John Lennon's murder hit him hard, and he traveled to New York to attend a vigil. While he was there, as sort of a memorial to Lennon, he did a speed painting of Lennon at the vigil. People were amazed. Outside of the confines of a chain restaurant, his work was seen as something innovative and pure. The trip to New York changed Dent's life. Eventually, he gave performances that he called his "Two-Fisted Art Attack." He painted with both hands and played music while he painted. He could finish a painting in three songs. He was unique, and what he produced was remarkable considering the way he produced it.

Dent died in 2004, and I bought his paintings while he was still alive. Art is such a weird thing, because you end up with a much more valuable piece after someone dies. That's a creepy thing to profit from, but it's true nonetheless.

I think I paid $1,000 for the Morrison painting, and right now it's listed as "Not For Sale" in the shop. The other one is yours for $30,000.

There was a time when I had three Dent paintings. The third, a portrait of Jimi Hendrix, came off pawn one day in the summer of 2010 and it was purchased the day it came off. The buyer? I gave Chumlee a screaming deal and let him have it for $3,500. I can understand him liking the painting, but Chumlee being Chumlee, he's not being especially smart with his money.

WE USED TO HAVE a custom jewelry department in the pawn shop. We had jewelers who made jewelry to order, and it was quite an experience before we became too busy to keep it going. The most famous piece we made in the shop was a pimp's ring that was shaped like a king's crown. Back in the nineties, crown rings were all the rage among pimps. It was a sign of belonging to the club, because if you were wearing a crown ring you were announcing to everybody that you were, indeed, a pimp.

Well, the pimp who commissioned the crown ring wanted to be the pimpiest of pimps, because this ring was the most amazingly hideous thing you could imagine. It was like the crown on the Imperial margarine package. Each corner of the crown had a diamond coming off it, and it was *huge*. It was literally like wearing a shotglass on your finger.

Without a doubt, it was the gaudiest thing I ever saw in my life. We made it to his specifications, and we charged him $10,000.

The pimp ended up losing it in a pawn. He didn't claim it, so it came off pawn and I was left to deal with it. The only person in the world who would even consider putting this thing on his finger is a pimp. Every other human in the world would just laugh at it.

So I sold it to another pimp. The second pimp pawned it and lost it, so I sold it to another pimp. Same thing happened. This ring bounced pimp to pimp. It ended up being in and out of the shop for five years, and it found itself on the finger of at least five pimps.

At some point that nobody could determine, crown rings lost their cachet among pimps. They moved on to some other talisman of success, and I was left with a shotglass-sized pimp ring and no pimp to buy it. In other words, I was stuck with it. We tried and tried, but we were repeatedly turned down.

In the end, the most famous pimp ring in the history of Gold & Silver Pawn met its demise. We ended up scrapping it. But who knows? Its parts might have found themselves onto the fingers or necks of some other group of pimps somewhere. I guess you'd call it the ultimate in recycling.

HERE ARE A FEW more: The world's fastest motorcycle is a Suzuki Hayabusa GSXR 1300. These bikes go 200 mph and are the gold standard for speed-freak bikers. Somebody came into the shop about a year ago and sold us one, and word spread among the speed-freak bikers that we had a Hayabusa, and a guy came in and said he wanted to buy it. We have to wait thirty days before we sell something to make sure it doesn't come up stolen, so Corey told him he had to wait. He was a speed-freak guy who was also a member of a motorcycle club that was known for doing stunts on city streets and freeways, like doing stand-up wheelies down I-15 at 100 mph for two miles.

Corey told him, "I'll be glad to sell it to you after it clears."

The guy didn't want to miss out on this, so he told Corey, "OK, but let me put a deposit down on it right now." He handed Corey $10,000 on the spot and said he'd pay him the other $10,000 when the bike came off.

No problem, good deal for us, and the guy was planning a trip to the Bonneville Salt Flats to do some racing.

Before the thirty days passed, the guy was killed in a motorcycle accident that happened during one of his stunt rides. We're legally obligated to hold the merchandise for sixty days before someone forfeits their deposit, but we held this bike for six months waiting for someone from the family to come in and claim it. Nobody ever did, though, so after six months we put it back out for sale.

✳ ✳ ✳ ✳

DURING THE BUILDING BOOM in Las Vegas, a guy walked into the store and proceeded to tell us he had a connection that could get us DeWalt grinders. His uncle owned a tool company and he had storage sheds full of these things that needed to be moved. He over-ordered or something, but the guy had a story that he told pretty well.

This became an obsession for this guy. His whole life revolved around selling us these DeWalt grinders. He came into the store four and five times a day to pitch us on the idea of buying his DeWalt grinders. I was intrigued but wary at the same time, because construction supplies and tools often turn up stolen. I had no idea where he was getting this stuff.

I called the cops and told them the story and asked them if they had any reason to believe the grinders might be hot. They got back to me and said no. I asked them if they would come down to the shop and talk to this guy directly, and they sent a guy down while he was here.

Grinder Guy greets the cop like an old friend. They shake hands and talk and laugh. He repeats his story the same way he told it to me, the cop listens to him, asks him a few questions, shrugs his shoulders at me, shakes Grinder Guy's hand, and leaves the shop. Everything checks out.

Over the course of the next three months, I buy five hundred brand-new, still-in-the-box DeWalt grinders from this guy. Five hundred hand-held grinders, and during that time I could sell each and every one of them.

And then one day at the beginning of the fourth month, the cops come into the shop and say, "All those DeWalt grinders are hot." This is after I've done everything I can think to make sure I'm not getting stuck with stolen merchandise.

"Wait a second," I tell the cop. "You guys checked him out. I had you talk to him. What else could I do?"

"Yeah, I know, but the company he was working for didn't know they were missing until now. They just reported it."

* * * *

HERE'S HOW CHANGES AT the macro level of the economy can trickle down to the micro level:

About five years ago, Home Depot and Lowe's switched from selling American-made MK tile saws ($900 apiece) to Chinese-made saws ($200 to $250 apiece). The company that supplied the Chinese tile saws had to agree to buy all these MK tile saws off the shelves and inventory of Home Depot. And if you're selling a certain brand of saw, you can't also be carrying a different brand. To put it another way, if Ford was forced to buy up all the Chevys, Ford would want to get rid of the Chevys as quickly as possible, because they wouldn't want it to be known that they were holding both brands.

I had done a little bit of business with this company that made the Chinese tile saws; I got some saws cheaply and sold them on the Internet. One of the guys who was a contact with that company called me up to tell me the Chinese company was going to be looking to unload all these MK tile saws for a pretty good price, as long as they could be promised that I would buy them all. I agreed, then negotiated the price: $125 apiece for brand-new MK tile saws that had been selling the previous day for $900 at Home Depot.

I *sort of* knew what I was getting into, but it's hard to visualize three semi loads full of tile saws. Well, the semis showed up at the pawn shop, and after we filled up every available space in the shop—which wasn't that much—we moved on to the other buildings I own that are adjacent to the shop. We filled every available space in those, too—and we still had two full semis sitting in the parking lot.

The next stop was my house. We filled my garage with MK tile saws. We filled Corey's garage with MK tile saws. We filled my aunt's garage with MK tile saws. When Tracy came home from the store that day, she almost had to walk sideways to get into the house.

(And the kicker: On the day when I could finally move the saws out of my garage, which might have qualified as one of the happiest days of Tracy's life, I moved some of them only to find that a family of rattlesnakes had decided to make its nest at the bottom of one of the pallets. So not only did I have a garage full of tile saws, but I was also providing a home for rattlesnakes.)

I sold the saws for $400 apiece, and this was back when there was a ton of construction in town. I sold them for $300 to guys who sold them in swap meets all over California. I sold them over the Internet. I sold them on the showroom floor. I'd pay guys that work for me to take them out to the local swap meets and sell them. Wherever you could imagine buying or selling a tile saw, I was there.

The beautiful thing was, the Chinese company had to agree to take all the returns from Lowe's and Home Depot. If someone returned one after the stores stopped carrying them, they were sent directly to the Chinese company. And when they came to me and asked if I was willing to take on the returns as well, I said, "Sure—for $25 each."

They agreed, and I hired two guys whose sole job it was to stand out in the back lot and fix these returned MK tile saws. Sometimes there was a piece missing, or a blade broke, or something simple. They were out there swapping out parts and fixing saws. A lot of times people buy a tile saw, do a quick job, clean it up, and return it. They might tell the store there's something wrong with it, but there isn't—they just don't need it any longer so they take it back and figure Home Depot can deal with it.

You might not expect to find new tile saws at a pawn shop on Las Vegas Boulevard. Then again, you might not expect to find $30,000 paintings or a ring the size of a shotglass. (You might not expect to find that anywhere, probably.) I'm always getting calls from people with connections, and I'm always willing to listen. I might not always jump in, but if there's a deal—and a buck—to be made, I'm there. That's another one of the lessons of the pawn shop: There's a market for *everything*.

RESEARCH IN ACTION

MY IDEAS DON'T ALWAYS WORK. Maybe it's equal parts fearlessness and arrogance, but I've never embarked on one without completely believing it would succeed. I've always looked at the conventional ways in which business is transacted—the payday loan business is a good example—and tried to turn it on its head. If there's an alternative route to the same destination, I'm willing to take it.

This holds true for big endeavors and small. One of the most unusual, and potentially dangerous, ideas I came up with in the nineties was to refine my own gold from our jewelry department. Here's how it works: Every time you get your gold jewelry cleaned, a little bit of gold comes off. A busy jewelry store will polish off a lot of gold every day, and every jewelry store has a very expensive buffing machine with filters and vacuums on it to collect the residue. There's a practical reason for this: For every pound of used buffing powder, you can reclaim anywhere from a quarter ounce to an ounce of pure gold.

At the time, I was selling our bags of powder for seventy-five bucks each. As you can see, there's a reason a good jewelry store will always offer to clean your jewelry: It's money in the bank. And the harder the buffing compound, the more gold will come off.

Rick being Rick, I read a book on refining gold. I developed my own buffing compound, and I found out there's a lot more gold left in buffing powder than they say there is. I was getting screwed at seventy-five bucks a bag all those years. So from there I took the logical next step: I went around buying everybody's buffing compound.

I didn't have the same kind of lab equipment the pros had. I was going by the seat of my pants, learning chemistry by reading a book. I probably had $500 worth of lab equipment when I should have had $20,000. When I first started, I remember I'm in the garage refining my gold and I'm nearly passing out in the middle of a cloud of blue smoke. So I went to the book, flipped through a few pages, and found the problem. "OK, I get it. I didn't get all the nitric acid out of the solution."

This process creates a lot of toxic waste that needs proper disposal. For the limited amount of gold I was refining, it got too expensive to get rid of the waste, so I had to quit after a year. I'm glad I did it, though. After all, if you're going to read all those science books, you might as well try out the science inside them, right?

My reading list looks more like the typical mad professor's than a pawn shop owner's. I've read all four volumes of Asimov's *Understanding Physics*, and each volume is dog-eared and annotated. Some of the more interesting books I've read in the past couple of years include: *Diagnosis: Mercury*, about the history of mercury poisoning; *The Battery: How Portable Power Sparked a Technological Revolution*; *Thirteen Things That Don't Make Sense: The Most Baffling Scientific Mysteries of Our Time*; *Professor Stewart's Cabinet of Mathematical Curiosities*; *The Ten Most Beautiful Experiments*; *Against the Gods: The Remarkable Story of Risk*; and *The Monty Hall Problem: The Remarkable Story of History's Most Contentious Brain Teaser*.

I'm not a passive consumer, either. When Corey was about thirteen, he came into the garage during my cold fusion stage of lab work. You read that right: cold fusion. This was back when it was the craze, making its way onto the cover of *Time* magazine as the newest form of cheap energy. Cold fusion was supposed to create more energy than you needed to put into creating it. Again, I bought a book and read about it, and I came away thinking I could do it. Well, Corey walked in one day, took a look at me, slammed the door, and ran into the house yelling to Tracy, "Mom, Dad's doing some weird shit in the garage."

Just then, they hear *Boom!* Near as I could figure, slamming the door separated the palladium from the hydrogen sulfide in my jar. I got a mushroom cloud. I swear to God it was working—I was on my way to successful cold fusion—when Tracy pulled the plug on me because she was convinced I was going to blow up the house and everything in it.

Of course, I was convinced I was a few steps away from making it happen. It's similar to the feeling I had a year before we got the television show, when I was equally sure I had discovered the world's greatest loophole, and it was going to allow me to get filthy rich off nickels.

Yes, nickels.

Hear me out.

First, a little background: There is money lurking in the strangest places. The catalytic converter in your car is full of precious metals. Catalytic converter production is the largest market for platinum, and a converter in a large eight-cylinder car has two grams of platinum inside. A small amount—probably a quarter gram—of rhodium is in there as well. At the peak of the metals boom, rhodium was $10,000 an ounce. People who knew this were crawling under their cars with a Sawzall and cutting the catalytic converters out. Prices have come down since then, but if the catalytic converter in your car needs to be replaced, make sure you get your old one. A junkyard will give you $75 to $80 for it.

Back to the nickels: At the time I devised my scheme, the price of nickel had risen to twenty dollars a pound. Copper was $4.50 a pound.

A nickel scrapped for ten cents.

I went out and bought $10,000 worth of nickels, hoping to scrap them for eight cents apiece. That's more than a 40 percent margin for a product that's easy to get, and I considered that pretty much a foolproof deal.

I would go into a bank and ask for $100 worth of nickels. I would go into another bank and do the same thing. I had my employees go into banks to get $100 worth of nickels. I went to vending machine companies and told them I'd buy all of their nickels. I bought so many nickels I had one of the employees at the shop load down a one-ton pickup with nickels. When they went to move the truck, the bed was sitting on the tires. There were too many nickels for the truck to hold.

Hey, they make something like a billion nickels a year; I just wanted a quarter of them.

And I found someone to buy them. I found a scrap dealer in California. I told him what I had and the guy said, "I'll take all you've got." Well, this happened about a week before Congress passed a law that outlawed scrapping nickels. Just my luck—Congress figured out it cost the mint thirteen cents to make a nickel, and they knew people were catching on to it.

Now I'm sitting there with a ton and a half of nickels and nothing to do with them. Now they're all just worth five cents, not eight. There's no margin in these nickels.

So I reversed the process. Every day I would walk into the bank and get a $100 bill for a bag of nickels. I don't know—some of the bags still might be being used as doorstops in the back room of the pawn shop. God only knows what lurks in some of those darker corners.

Now it's a felony in the United States to take more than five dollars' worth of nickels out of the country. So much for my plan.

IN MY BUSINESS, I have to be familiar with a lot of arcane and mind-boggling laws. For instance, I bet you didn't know that every single transaction that takes place at a pawn shop gets downloaded to Homeland Security, did you? It does—it's a little-known clause in the Patriot Act.

Another one relates to the sale of firearms. I sell guns, but only antique guns, those that were made in 1898 or before. Federal regulations for antique guns are vastly different from those governing non-antique guns, and in a lot of ways the laws are completely nonsensical.

I have an 1895 .45-caliber pistol in my shop. You can put modern ammunition in it and it's a deadly weapon, but it's exempt from the strict regulations that cover non-antique guns. I don't care how old it is, you could use it right now and it's as lethal as a brand-new Glock. And if you want that 1895 gun, you can walk into the shop and buy it from me without an ID and without a waiting period. As far as the federal government is concerned, it's scrap metal.

If you try to buy the world's worst piece-of-shit .25-caliber handgun, it's a three-day waiting period and a ton of taxes and a mountain of paperwork. But you can go out and buy a fully functional 1898 Gatling gun without someone even asking you your name. And not only that, but any muzzle-loading weapon of any vintage can be purchased without paperwork of any kind. They're considered antiques, or at least antiquated, and they've fallen through the cracks of the weapons laws. In fact, I have a mortar in the shop that can fire a bowling ball over a mile, and because it's muzzle-loaded, it's yours without any required paperwork or a waiting period. Buy it today, roll it out of the shop, and fire it to your heart's content. It's nothing short of insane.

Weird contradictions, especially in government, have always fascinated me. Partly because of these odd gun laws, I read a book about strange laws. One of the passages typifies what I find to be true today: In the 1700s in England a guy walking down the street yelled at someone across the way, "Thoust are a thief. Thoust has stolen my dung."

The guy who was accused of stealing took the accuser to court, citing slander. His argument was that dung is real property and therefore cannot be stolen, hence the slander. English common law differentiated between personal property and real property, and real property was considered "property of the land" or what we would consider real estate. The judge listened to both sides and then ruled in one of the most confusing ways imaginable.

In the end, he decided this: If the dung was piled—in other words, placed in organized piles—then it was personal property, but if it was spread across the land it was real property.

Clearly, the United States isn't immune from quirky laws. Take Prohibition, which produced some of the best law-breaking stories in the history of our country. I have a few bottles of medicinal whiskey that were produced during Prohibition. They're rare and unusual, so they're worth quite a bit of money to the right person. In truth, they're not really bottles; they're more like metal containers, similar to lighter-fluid cans.

During Prohibition, you had to have a prescription to get whiskey. On the side of the container it says, "Recommended by physicians and surgeons." On the front it says, "Strictly for medicinal purposes."

I'm not sure whether alcoholism was considered a medical condition that necessitated a prescription for grain alcohol, but I'm guessing it was. Just looking at that container and reading the restrictions and conditions fascinates me. It really wasn't that long ago, in a historical sense, that people were dealing with that.

And part of what I love about looking at something like the medicinal whiskey is thinking about how many different directions it can lead. There are a million tributaries that flow from each item, and each item has both a narrower and a broader story that tells something about our culture at the time.

There's a great Prohibition story about Charles Lindbergh. He was coming to visit San Francisco, and apparently he enjoyed a glass or two of wine. The mayor of San Francisco at the time sent some cops to Napa to get some communion wine from the famous Christian Brothers Winery, since communion (or altar) wine was the only alcohol that was legal at the time. They drove a paddy wagon and headed north from the city to load up on wine for a big dinner commemorating Lindbergh's visit. They figured a few cases of wine would do the job.

When the cops arrived, the winery refused to sell them any wine at all. The brothers told them there were rules to follow to make sure the winery didn't get in trouble with the feds. They outlined what the cops would have to do in order to be eligible to purchase wine.

First, they had to have a note from a priest. Second, every person with a note from a priest would be entitled to purchase three bottles of wine and three bottles only.

The cops returned to San Francisco with the bad news. The mayor regrouped, and the next day there was a line of a hundred cops outside Christian Brothers Winery, each holding a note from a priest.

Some of the weird laws make sense. It's been a dozen years since someone tried to sell me dental gold that looks gray and ashy, but I've had more than a few people try it since I've been working in the shop. Those people get a quick response: Get the hell out. It's a felony to sell or buy crematory gold. It's another weird, obscure law, the kind that makes you wonder what events took place to necessitate such a law in the first place.

And then again, some things are best left unconsidered.

AS I'VE SAID, TELEVISION has taken away some of the one-on-one contact I have with my customers. It was an unavoidable by-product of the visibility, but it is a downside. It's a little less personal these days.

There are exceptions, though, and one of them is a big-time sports gambler I'll call David. He lives for the NFL season, and he has a routine he follows for the NFL games every weekend. He bets five-team parleys for $2,000, and he always takes the Monday night game.

The odds on a five-team are about 50:1, so it's a $100,000 ticket for him if it hits. Being the degenerate gambler he is, he rolls in on Monday morning, broke off his ass, but he's already hit four teams on a five-team ticket.

He also knows the power of ready cash, which is what I have and what he needs.

"Hey, Rick, can I borrow fifty grand to back up my bet?"

He's hedging here. He'll bet the other side in the game that night, knowing he's going to win either way. And if I lend him the money, I know I'm going to win either way, too. So I'll take parley tickets as collateral. I see the ticket, I double-check all the scores to make sure he's right, and I go down to the window with him to place the $50,000 bet myself. The money never leaves my hands, and I hold all the tickets until the bet is settled.

The next day I will go down to the casino, go to the window, and collect the money. I don't care who wins. If the hedge bet wins, he'll pay me back my $50,000 plus the 10 percent vig. I'm making five grand either way. He's making money either way. With long days of filming and constant demands on my time, it's inevitable that some of that personal touch gets lost in the mix. But if David walks in next Monday morning one win away from a five-team parley, asking for $50,000, one of the guys at the counter better come and get me.

THE GUYS WORKING NIGHT shift have their hands full. They cope. I worked the night shift on and off for the first ten years we had the shop. We couldn't afford to pay more employees, so we had to take turns doing the work. It's amazing how bold people get when they're drunk and there's a couple inches of bulletproof glass separating you from them. I guarantee you I hold some kind of record for most times being told to fuck off. I'd put my record up against anybody on that statistic.

There's another statistic I wish I'd kept track of: The number of times I was offered sex in exchange for some money out of the pawn-shop coffers. This is a good one, because imagine for a moment the type of woman who would walk up to a pawn-shop window in Las Vegas in the middle of the night and offer the guy behind the window sex. I've had women offer to give me a blow job for two bucks.

I have a standard reply, too.

"Sorry, ma'am, I have a two-tooth minimum."

You really can't get mad at these people, even the ones who get pissed when you refuse them. You just have to laugh and accept them for the idiots they are.

The basic fact is this: If you're working the window in the middle of the night, you're the party-stopper. You're the asshole behind the window saying no. You might as well be a cop rolling up on them, because they come in thinking you're their friend only to walk away thinking you're part of the authoritarian regime or some such crap. I won't apologize for that, because if you're out partying on a Sunday morning at 3 A.M. and the pawn shop is the only place you can get cash, you should probably just go home.

I don't deal with drunk people. That's just a basic rule. This doesn't always go over very well, that's for sure. When people come up and I say, "No, I can't give you any money for that tonight," they get pissed. Very pissed. Loud and pissed.

And then when I say, "You're drunk, I'm not dealing with you," they take it up to a whole new level of pissed. I won't budge, though, and I tell my employees the same thing. It might reduce business, but if they're blatantly drunk I don't believe it's morally right for me to be complicit in their behavior. If you're not in your right mind and you're trying to sell me something, especially something that's been in your family for generations, I'm guessing I stand a pretty good chance of being sued when you sober up.

God knows I've been sued for everything else in the world, so I'm not interested in taking my chances with a drunk guy selling a family heirloom to get a few more drinks. Or, more likely, being sued by members of his family when they realize Mr. Black Sheep sold great-grandma's silver tea set to get another bottle of Hennessy.

There are different ways to cope sitting in there all night. Chumlee had his dog, a sixty-pound pit bull named Nevada, for companionship and protection. Other guys sit bug-eyed staring out the window, waiting for the next show to start.

For many years I had a camera setup that allowed me to see what was going on at the window from home. We have regular customers who pawn expensive jewelry, and sometimes their schedules don't coincide with mine. The cameras allowed me to look at the items people bring to the night window to ask for more money than the night shift can access. I'm in bed reading at eight most nights, while they could be wandering up to the night window at three looking to get twenty grand for pawning some expensive jewelry.

My night guys don't have access to that kind of dough. I trust them, but . . .

Put it this way: You've got one guy in the store with ten grand in cash and everything you own in the world sitting there. It's a good thing we have guns behind the counter and Las Vegas Metro less than three minutes away every time we hit the panic button.

(If we accidentally hit the panic button, Las Vegas Metro is there in three minutes. This has happened four or five times over the past twenty years, and Metro has to respond the same whether the alarm is tripped accidentally or not, since they have no way of being sure. When the button gets pushed, a call immediately comes in from the police. "This is Metro, are you being robbed?" "No, it was an accident." "OK, what are you wearing?" The guy says, "Black Gold & Silver Pawn polo, jeans, Nikes." "OK, come out of the store with your hands up, we don't want to see any guns." This is a pawn shop, so they know we've got guns on hand. The guy will walk out the front door and there will be cops with shotguns drawn around every corner. It might be a little scary, but that's the price you pay for pushing the damned button.)

There was a woman who was always losing her ass gambling, and she had some rings and necklaces that she regularly pawned when she got low. They'd call me up and I'd ask, "OK, you got the rubies?" And the night guy would hold them up. "You got the diamonds?" He'd hold them up. This was stuff I'd seen a hundred times before, so I just needed to know she had them with her before I headed down there to get the money.

I can't count the number of times I got a call in the middle of the night to look at the cameras to assess someone's stuff. Then if it was legit, I'd get dressed, drive to the shop, and handle the transaction myself.

I stopped doing that a few years ago, though. Now it's Corey's job. He's had to get up from a dinner in a restaurant and tell his wife, "Got to go. You pay the bill." Everything in the family trickles downward, the way it's supposed to.

WE TOOK A TRIP to Hawaii in September of '01, and we got stuck there when the planes stopped flying after 9/11. Rick being Rick, as Tracy would say, we spent a lot of time roaming swap meets while we were on the island of Oahu.

There's a huge swap meet in the parking lot of Aloha Stadium, and I was in heaven just walking around trying to find stuff that I could bring back home. (I also wanted to do some surfing, so I bought a surfboard off a kid for $15. It was cheaper than renting one.) I was amazed to find a guy at one booth selling Hawaii emergency money.

The back story: During World War II, the massive troop buildup in Hawaii after Pearl Harbor created a massive shortage of money. There was still a great fear that Hawaii was going to be invaded by the Japanese, so the government took steps to protect U.S. currency in the event Japan took over Hawaii. The government didn't want Japan to have the ability to reuse the money, so it created a system where Hawaii used a separate currency from the rest of the country. These bills had a big stamp on them—"HAWAII"—that kept them from circulating with normal U.S. currency. If Hawaii was invaded, the government could immediately announce that all those bills were null and void.

After the war, those bills were recalled, but some of them pop up now and again. I got a $20 bill for $30, and I sold it back at the shop for $200. It never hurts to look around. I never know what's going to walk through my door, but I also never know what I'm going to walk into if I take the time to look around.

MY BUDDY DAVE KNUCKLES worked for me for a while. He was the best man in my wedding to Tracy, and he was a character. One day he was working the night window and a guy tried to pawn a plaster of Paris monkey head. The thing was worthless, maybe less than worthless, but the guy was only asking for $10 so Dave thought what the hell. It would make a good story, anyway.

Well, a few weeks later the guy paid the pawn and picked it up. Probably the most ridiculous thing anybody ever repaid a loan—with interest—to pick up.

We had one dumbass employee who bought about $5,000 worth of DeWalt tools. The customer had a line of credit with Home Depot and he was short on cash. This was his scheme: He was going to buy tools at Home Depot with his line of credit and sell them to us without even opening them.

The employee takes the first three tools and checks them out—they're good. We have rules on whatever we get. You've got to test it, which means making sure it works. Plug it in, turn the crank, whatever you need to do. Well, he tests these tools and sees the box is still sealed, the tools are intact, everything looks good.

The guy keeps coming back with more and more tools. He's apparently going to Home Depot every day to buy tools. The employee keeps buying them, but by now he's just carrying the boxes into the back room and handing the guy his money.

Corey went into the back room and started organizing these tools, and he opened more than a dozen boxes that had nothing but bricks in them. We got fleeced by this guy—for $5,000—because our employee couldn't be bothered to open the damned boxes.

WE HAVE A WAY of dealing with people who steal things. Corey's pretty good at stuff like this, and one day someone reached over the counter and stole a Rolex. We caught him red-handed, dead to rights, stealing a Rolex out of the case.

It's one of those things where you can call the cops. They're going to give the guy a ticket or take him to jail. If they press charges, he's not going to show up in court. This whole ordeal is likely to waste six months of my life.

Someone in the shop—I won't say who—asked the guy, "So, you want an ass-beating or you want to go to jail?"

Well, any self-respecting criminal will take the ass-beating any time. This guy was no exception. So this unnamed employee walks up on him and spits in his face. Then the unnamed employee says, "Wipe that off your face and I'll break your nose."

The guy just stands there, and the unnamed employee says, "OK, now give me your driver's license or ID." The guy starts hemming and hawing—"No, don't do that." The employee looks at him like he's going to make good on his promise to break the guy's nose, so the guy reaches into his wallet and gives him his driver's license.

The employee calmly walks behind the counter, to the wall near where Old Man sits, and pins the driver's license to the wall.

"Oh, no, man," the Rolex-stealer says. "You can't do that."

"I can't? Why don't you call the cops and tell them that?"

"Oh, man, now you're going to make me go to the DMV?"

We figure it's worse to go to the DMV for six hours to get an ID than it is to go to jail. Most of the guys we've caught stealing seem to agree.

RICK'S RULES
OF NEGOTIATION

1. **YOU'VE GOT TO BE ABLE TO WALK AWAY:** You can't fall in love with something. You can't decide that you're going to buy this thing no matter what because you've decided you can't live without it. Negotiating to purchase an item should not be an emotional process. It's analytical, and a lot of factors have to be considered in a short amount of time. I have to consider how long it's going to take me to sell it, how big the potential market for it is, how much I can reasonably expect to get for it. It goes well beyond saying, "It's worth a thousand dollars and he'll take five hundred, so I have to buy it."

2. **IT'S JUST STUFF:** You *can* live without it. You have up to this point in your life, so there's no reason to believe you can't go on living a happy and fulfilling life without the thing that's sitting in front of you. There are many times when I've come across something that I really, really wanted, but that little voice in my head keeps repeating those three magic words: It's. Just. Stuff. And you know what? It is. It's just disposable, superficial stuff. Some of it's really cool, though, so you have to be careful.

3. **DON'T TIP YOUR HAND:** If you can tell from the moment you start talking price that the other person is going to capitulate, there are no negotiations. Rule No. 1 applies to both the buyer and

the seller. If the seller shows he is not willing to walk away, if he in-dicates through body language or words that he absolutely has to get this done, he's yours. He's also lost money.

4. **NEVER GIVE THE FIRST NUMBER:** After the story has been established, it's time to move on to price. The preemptive question is always the same: "What are you looking to get out of it?" Get their number first. Information is power, and getting this information first is extremely powerful. It allows you to know whether the person knows what he has and whether he's realistic about what he can get for it. As a buyer, you don't want to run the risk of coming in first with a high price. You might be telling the other guy something about his item that he doesn't know, and it's important to remember that it's not your job to educate the customer. It's his stuff, and it's his job to do the research that gives him the best chance to maximize his profits. At all costs, get their number first.

5. **NEVER HAVE A HARSH NEGOTIATION:** Laugh, joke around, be their friend. Engage them in the item—that's why I always ask for the story behind it. I want to get some personal information out of the seller and a better feel for where the seller is coming from. That allows me to play off the information—family history, etc.—and make him or her feel more comfortable. If you're joking and laughing, you're their friend. Then when it comes to negotiating a price, it's no longer simply a business proposition. The tone changes. Now it's more like "Hey, help a buddy out." And they'll feel better about taking less.

One of the best ways to learn how to negotiate is to study it. I'm always the buyer on the television show, but I have spent my share of time on the other side of the counter. It's not as much fun, I can tell you that.

I have made many trips to the diamond district in L.A. to sell my diamonds. If I find myself in possession of a very large or valuable diamond, I have no choice but to head to L.A. and negotiate with the best there is. And there is no doubt who owns that title: The Hasidic Jews in the diamond district are the best negotiators in the world.

They will look at a diamond for three hours. They can learn everything in the world they need to know about the diamond in three minutes. They're smart; they do this all day and they do it better than anyone. Doesn't matter. They look for any angle or edge they can get, and then they exploit it until you show them you are either going to hold your ground or cave in.

The Gemological Institute of America provides the ratings for diamonds, and the GIA is the absolute gold standard in the business. What they say goes. If you have anyone but the GIA grade your diamond, the grade you get is worthless. The GIA rules.

Well, not always. I have had the guys in the diamond district argue with me about GIA ratings. They know I have no counter to their argument except to say, "Come on, dude—it's the GIA." They don't care. They don't care at all. If you falter or don't know your stuff, you're done. They will eat you alive.

It's like a hostage situation. They're the most patient people I've ever encountered, and they will always wait you out. I've learned a lot from them, although my tactics might be a little different. For one thing, they surely aren't interested in Rule #5, the one about making sure every negotiation is a friendly one. That's not their game.

I had a diamond that was D-VVS I, which meant it was one grade away from flawless. The GIA rating sheet included cutting instructions on how to make it flawless. I sent it to a local diamond cutter and sent it back to GIA and they said it still wasn't flawless. I had him cut it again and they said it *still* wasn't flawless.

OK, so now I'm $14,000 into this one diamond, and I'm getting a little pissed off. Every time it gets cut it takes a little off the diamond, too, and diamonds are priced by the ounce. So I'm losing every which way on this diamond that might be the most amazing and perfect diamond I will ever see.

I took it to Los Angeles and went through two days of negotiations. I was dealing with three different guys. I dealt with the first guy for six hours. Six hours. And another was three hours. And then the third was six more hours. That type of negotiation is based on one thing: time.

They look at you and say, "I'll give you a hundred dollars."

"No, that's not going to work."

"OK, let me look at it again."

So they take it back, roll it over in their hands for about ten minutes, and then say, "I'll give you a hundred dollars."

"I told you, that's not going to work."

"OK, let me look at it again. . . . . I'll give you a hundred dollars."

It's endless, and it's tedious, but damn if it isn't effective. I've been in there and said, "I need to use a restroom."

"Sorry, we don't have one."

"Wait, you don't have a restroom on this entire floor?"

"No, we don't."

So you're standing there, knowing they're messing with you to get the diamond for the price they want to pay. You don't want to give in, but the reality of the situation is, you have to pee. It's like a hostage negotiation with these guys. They know all the tricks, and they'll use them without a second thought. Their job is to get what they want for the least amount possible, and damned if they aren't great at it.

They come into our shop, too. I'll deal with them, Corey will deal with them, and I've had Tracy deal with them. (She even told one of them we didn't have a restroom after hearing my stories.) But if they show up and Old Man is behind the counter, he kicks them out.

A diamond dealer walks in to talk to Old Man, they're gone. He knows how good they are, and he knows he doesn't have the patience to deal with them. If you know you can't win, sometimes it's best not to play the game.

IF YOU'RE NOT FAMILIAR with the pawn business and you watch *Pawn Stars*, you might come away with the impression that we never give people enough money for their stuff. It's a common complaint: Someone comes into the shop with a rare and unusual item, they say they want $4,000 for it, and they end up walking out with half that. If they say they saw it for $4,500 on eBay, people believe that's what it's worth and in the end I look like I'm cheating someone.

For one thing, telling me what someone is asking for an item on eBay doesn't mean anything to me. I've made millions of dollars in eBay sales, so I know you can ask anything you want on eBay. You can put a Happy Meal toy on eBay for $10,000, but that doesn't mean you should come into my shop and tell me you have the exact same Happy Meal toy and you're looking to get $10,000 for it.

The first thing I have to consider when I'm looking at a piece is how long it's going to take to resell it. It might be the coolest thing in the world, but if it's going to take three or four years to sell, its value immediately decreases for my purposes. There are times when someone brings me an antique firearm that I know I can turn around and sell immediately to someone in my network of collectors. In that case, I'll be willing to pay more money. But if it's something I can't sell immediately, I'm less willing to part with top dollar just to have it in the shop.

There are different rules for regular items and commodities. If someone walks in with a handful of Krugerrands (South African one-ounce gold pieces), they don't have to be held for thirty days. They don't have serial numbers like currency, so there's really no way of telling whether they're stolen or not. And gold is one of the few guarantees in this business. I can sell them the next day, and there will always be a market for them.

The price of gold as I write is $1,340 an ounce. We routinely pay $1,300 for a Krugerrand and make forty bucks because it's a guaranteed sale.

I don't have that with some weird antiques or a Picasso or a Denny Dent painting of Jim Morrison. I have to be smart about something like that, because I look at it and factor in how long it's going to take me to sell the thing. So if I think I can eventually get three thousand for it, you're getting twelve hundred. If it takes me three to five years to sell it, I'm not going to give you an auction-house price on it.

I hear it all the time. *You're giving those people almost nothing for their stuff. If something's worth five thousand bucks, how can you justify giving them only two thousand? You're fleecing people.*

It works the other way, too. There are times when I will look at an item and mentally prepare myself to pay ten thousand bucks. I saunter up to the customer, smile, and say, "Hey, there. What are you looking to get out of this?"

And they say, "Oh, man, I'd really like to get nine hundred bucks."

So that's another moral dilemma. Most of the time I don't believe it's my job to educate the seller on his or her property, but there are times when my conscience gets the best of me. Once—and we used this on a show—a woman came in with a one-of-a-kind Fabergé spider. Given the age and the amazing quality of the work, I believe it was made by Peter Fabergé himself.

She had no idea she was holding an item that could be worth upward of $20,000. No idea at all. I looked at her and laughed a little, but I came clean. She was thinking it might be worth $1,000, but she was even flimsy with that. When I outlined the history and rarity of it, her eyes kept getting bigger and bigger.

She left the shop with twelve grand in her pocket after coming in with no expectations. She was a lot happier walking out than walking in.

People are free to think what they want about me and my business, but remember this: I have to make a profit, and I have to figure out the best way to make a profit. And if you don't want to accept two thousand for your five-thousand-dollar painting, you're free to walk out that door with it under your arm.

I always say I never know what's going to come through that door, and the opposite is true, too: I never know what's going to walk *out* that door, either.

BIG HOSS

NEVER THOUGHT MY LIFE WAS VERY IN-
teresting until we got a television show. Until then, I was
just a big dude rolling through life, working for my dad and
my grandpa in a pawn shop in Vegas. Then TV shows up
and everything changes. I guess I'm interesting now.

A pawn shop used to be the last place anybody wanted to end up in
Vegas. Think about it: Anywhere but there, right? If you found yourself
in a pawn shop, either something went horribly wrong or you were desperate. Neither one is a good outcome.

Thanks to television and a store full of unique and unusual items,
we've come a long way. It's crazy—now we're a tourist destination. People
get off the plane and come directly to the shop. We're mainstream now.
The first mainstream pawn shop. It makes me shake my head just thinking about it.

I have an assistant. That's the craziest thing I've ever heard. I have a
personal assistant who helps me keep my schedule straight and sets up
stuff around my house. If we need a new refrigerator, I send him over to
my house to wait for it. It's a different world now. If you had told me
three or four years ago that I'd have a personal assistant, I would have
laughed at you.

No, that's not completely correct. I wouldn't have laughed at you. Laughing means I would have thought it was a possibility. Instead, I think I would have looked at you like you were crazy, because that's what you would have been. Bat-shit crazy.

I SPENT THE BIGGEST part of my teenage years as a nasty drug addict. From the time I was fifteen till just after my twentieth birthday in 2003, I couldn't have been farther from the world I'm living in now. There was no money, no fame, no glamour.

Crystal meth is the worst shit in the world. It's the nastiest, meanest, most insidious drug ever invented. It swept through Las Vegas like a hot wind and picked up a ton of people along the way.

Ruined a lot of lives.

Almost ruined mine.

I can't really pinpoint how or why I started using. It didn't really seem like a considered decision on my part. When I was growing up, there wasn't always a lot of money flowing through our house. My dad and grandpa worked hard and long to make Gold & Silver Pawn a profitable enterprise, but there weren't always television cameras watching them peel off stacks of hundreds to buy rare and valuable items. Put it this way: Growing up, we ate English muffins for dinner more than once. We lived in a blue-collar neighborhood, where both parents had to work to make ends meet. My dad worked constantly, and while I was growing up my mom—she's not my biological mom, but Tracy is my real mom—worked the counter in the shop with him.

And it just seems like I woke up one day and everybody I hung out with was doing meth. Chumlee was one of my best buds in the neighborhood— he started doing it. My brother, Adam, started doing it. And so did I.

Once meth hit, it hit big. It ran through my neighborhood and my friends and people my age in a way that nobody could have guessed. It created a whole generation of people who engaged in what I call "face gymnastics." Their lips and cheeks and noses twitched and twisted constantly, as if they were swishing something around in their mouths or trying to stop an itch without using their hands.

I can tell when tweakers walk into the shop—and, believe me, a lot of them do—by watching how their faces move. Back, forth, up, down. That's before they open their toothless mouths and remove all doubt.

What a terrible life. I couch-surfed through life for those five years, living here and there, often not knowing where I was going to end up from night to night. I slept in a friend's trailer or in my truck or not at all. I stayed awake for two straight weeks one time. It should have been enough to kill me, but it wasn't.

Those two weeks are like a black hole in my memory. You'd think it would be easy to remember something that epic—a two-week binge with no sleep?—but I can't. It wasn't a social time. It was demented and depraved and sad. That whole time in my life is like a blur. I don't remember details, only broad outlines of what I did and where I was. It's like you lose time. I would sit in that trailer and do meth nonstop, the whole time wondering when and where we could get more. I had nothing, I did nothing, I was nothing.

My whole world revolved around the drug. I scoped out places to park my truck and sleep when I needed to. One day I found a car wash that gave me the perfect cover, and I thought it was a huge accomplishment. I could drive to the back behind the car-wash tunnel, lie across the front seat and sleep without anybody being able to see me. The way my life was at the time, that was a big score.

It's like crank was put on the earth for one reason: to make you want more. We did it just to do it, and after a while we'd do it just to feel normal. It became the new normal in my life, the one thing I could count on and understand. That's when you know it has completely taken over your life. It sinks its hooks into you and doesn't let go. You want to do it and don't care what the consequences are. You feel naked without it.

The rest of the world was drifting out of sight and out of mind, but meth was always there, front and center. It got to the point where I didn't know if it was pleasurable or not. I never gave it a second thought. All I knew was that I couldn't bear the thought of being without it.

It created gaps in my life. I woke up in jail not knowing how I got there. I woke up on the floor of a friend's trailer in the middle of the night one night because I felt something on my face. When I opened my eyes, all I could see was a girl with a demonic look. She was scratching at my face with both of her hands, convinced there were bugs crawling on me.

Another night I wasn't so lucky. I passed out in a house filled with tweakers and woke up the next morning looking like I came down with the worst case of chicken pox you ever saw. A girl that was there—not the same girl as before—swore my face had been crawling with bugs and it was her job to get rid of them. It looked like I'd been attacked with an ice pick. When you think about it, you have to ask yourself: What's the joy in doing a drug that makes you see bugs crawling on people's faces? Meth turns your life into an ongoing nightmare.

And it got expensive. Since I didn't have any money, this created problems. I had pretty much left home by the time I was seventeen, and my dad wasn't interested in supporting my bad habits. He didn't know what to do with me, just as his dad hadn't known what to do with him. He didn't enable me, though, the way many of my friends' parents did. He was not someone who was going to pat me on the back and tell me everything was going to be all right.

"You want to be a drug addict, fine," he told me. "Go be a drug addict out on the streets. You're not going to do it in my house, and you're not going to do it in the shop."

I went through some money, too. When I first became addicted, $25 would last me two or three days. Then it got to where I was blowing through a quarter ounce in two days—$800 worth. It was nonstop, a habit that closed off the rest of life. We'd sit in my buddy's trailer and get high, thinking and talking about how we were going to get more money to get more drugs and keep doing it. It was like throwing coal into a furnace. When we ran out of drugs, we'd go out on The Strip and steal, then use it to buy more drugs. Then, back to the trailer.

My entire life fit into a backpack.

Our big adventure was to go to a casino and play video poker. We were so stupid we did this even though we were too young to cash in. We could gamble, but we couldn't win. I was committing felonies to get high and gamble, and if I did happen to hit that royal flush . . . oh, well.

I had a strange attitude for being a drug addict. I knew that I was a drug addict and a piece of shit, but I also knew I wasn't always going to be one. I knew friends who stole from their parents and got so bad they didn't care about anybody or anything. In the back of my head, I knew there were people in my life I was going to have to eventually go back to and make amends. My dad was at the top of that list, so I never stole from him and I always tried to keep civil around him. It didn't always work, but there was that small, persistent part of me that knew I was going to make it out of this eventually.

My dad didn't know what to do with me, but he knew he had to do something. So he looked around and found a program called Job Corps. I was the first one to go there, followed by my brother, Adam, and then Chumlee. Over the course of about six months, my dad sent three of us there. They should have run a bus—the delinquent bus—from Vegas to Reno. We called Job Corps "Ghetto College," but it was a one-year trade school and one of the best programs out there. Chumlee and I were taught to be electricians and Adam became a plumber. My dad thought it would give us some direction and remove us from the influences in Vegas, which it did, but it also provided us with a little too much freedom. The students were what you'd call a diverse group—aimless guys like us, parolee gangbangers from Los Angeles, tough girls from Oakland and Sacramento. We kept using when we were there, kept screwing around on our off hours, although the program gave our lives some structure that they never had.

My other friends didn't have the same kind of support system. They had parents who just enabled them and made excuses for them. Their parents made it easy for them to continue to do drugs and feel sorry for themselves. Those are the guys who never turned it around. They never got that slap in the face or that wake-up call that let them know: (1) someone cared about them enough to make a hard decision; and (2) life couldn't go on indefinitely along the same hideous course.

Job Corps wasn't magic. Far from it. When we returned to Vegas, we fell back into the old cycle. My brother got a job as a plumber, and he did really well, but I wasn't much of an electrician. Chum went to work for McDonald's. We weren't exactly on the fast track to success.

Back to the drugs, too. Deep into them. After Reno I went on the two-week, no-sleep bender. After Reno I was still couch-surfing, still waking up wondering if someone tweaking harder than me would try to pick apart my face on those nights when I did sleep.

One night after Reno I was out with some people and I saw a bunch of girls in a parking lot in my dad's car. I'd been awake for several days and was in my typical state—high on meth. I flew into a rage and headed over to the car and started pulling them out of it, one by one.

"You stole my dad's car!" I kept yelling.

They were freaking out. During this scene, someone called the cops. I was handcuffed and thrown into the back of the squad car, and only then did I realize, somewhere deep in the recesses of my addled brain, that it wasn't my dad's car after all. I was either hallucinating or so far gone I couldn't see straight. Either way, the result was the same: I was assaulting a bunch of girls for being in a car that apparently looked like my dad's.

That earned me a night in jail. I didn't have many options when it came to calling someone to bail me out. My dad was disgusted with me at this point, so I called my grandmother on my biological mom's side to see if she might come down to the jail and bail me out. Usually guys like me have more luck with grandmas when they're in a situation like this. By some fluke, my mother was there, and she agreed to help me out.

For the first time in my life, I came upon something that made me believe there was a larger force at work in my life. You have to understand: I felt my mother was not around for me. I had a lot of problems with her for a lot of years.

But now, through some coincidence I'll never be able to adequately explain, she showed up at the Las Vegas jail to get her eighteen-year-old son. I hadn't seen her in six years. It wasn't the homecoming I envisioned, but she was there.

"I feel good," she told me. "It would make me feel better to be able to help you."

At this point, I was willing to take any help I could get. Something about the randomness of this encounter, the weirdness of her being there to help me when I really needed someone, made me think I was being given a sign from above: It was time to get clean, before it was too late.

She was living in Northern California, in Santa Rosa, and she suggested that I come back with her and try to get my act together there, away from Vegas, away from my friends, away from whatever trouble was consistently finding its way to me.

I agreed to go, with the intention of spending a couple of months getting sober and returning to Las Vegas.

Wishful thinking.

It wasn't that easy. Meth doesn't come with the same kind of physical withdrawals as heroin, but it's just as hard to quit. Your only desire is to do more, and you don't care what the consequences are. That's the hard part about quitting: When you're addicted, it's the only thing you want to do, so what is there without it?

My mom's house was across the street from a Carl's Jr. I told myself, "Every time I feel like getting high, I'm going to walk over to that Carl's Jr. and get a double-bacon western cheeseburger, a large fries, and a large Coke."

I felt like getting high *a lot*. How often? Put it this way: I gained 100 pounds in sixteen months. I was 230 pounds when I moved away from Vegas, and my dad liked to call me "the only fat tweaker in the history of the world." I got a lot fatter in the process of quitting, and the people at that Carl's Jr. got to watch me expand before their eyes.

But you know what? It gradually got easier. I wouldn't recommend that a double-bacon western cheeseburger replace a 12-step program, but it helped me. To each his own I guess.

After a few months, I got a job at a lumber mill in a town just north of Santa Rosa called Windsor. I worked for Calico Hardwoods, a company that makes stocks for rifles. The particulars of the job aren't that important—it was hard work, though—but to this point I had never had a job for more than two months.

As part of my recovery, when I started the job I told himself, "I don't care what happens, I don't care how bad of a job it is or how much I hate it, I've got to keep this job for at least a year."

I didn't enjoy my time in California. I was there for one reason: to get clean. I worked hard and stayed away from the drugs and ate a lot of double-bacon cheeseburgers. I didn't make friends or sightsee. I put my head down and injected some discipline into my life. After a while it became easier to put meth out of my mind, and by the time I left California I was the biggest anti-drug guy you'd ever want to know.

I worked at the mill for one year and one day. On that 366th day, I went into the office, quit my job, and moved back to Las Vegas, a hundred pounds heavier but way lighter in my soul.

CHUMLEE AND I HAVE been friends forever. (His real name is Austin Russell, but nobody ever calls him by his real name.) He's like a brother to me, maybe more than my real brother. We grew up in the same neighborhood, and he had some family problems that caused him to gravitate more and more toward our house. By the time he was ten or eleven, he was a fixture at our house at Thanksgiving and Christmas. I think he liked us, but I think food was a major attraction, too.

When I got back to Vegas after being in California, I made some calls to my old friends to see if any of them had gotten their acts cleaned up. I wasn't interested in hanging out with guys who were still using, and I was happy to hear Chum had gotten off the stuff, too. Most of the other guys were just walking clichés: dead or in jail. Chum was working in McDonald's and keeping his nose clean. I asked him if he wanted to go out and do something, and he said he couldn't afford it.

I knew he had gotten clean and was working and renting a small room from a guy, and I knew he didn't have any clothes or a car, so I was a little surprised he couldn't go out and do something. I mean, seriously—how much money does it cost to live like Chum? Plus, I wasn't looking to do something that would cost a lot of money, either. My tastes weren't very refined.

Then he ran it down for me. Working at McDonald's, it took a month's worth of paychecks for him to pay his rent, his food and his transportation to and from work. He was trying to make it work, and stay clean, and that's how he had to live. I respected that.

Around that same time, my dad got the bright idea to buy a Quiznos.

In order to open one of those, you have to work in one of them seven days a week for three weeks. Then you have to spend two weeks in Denver attending Quiznos University. For no pay.

There was no way my dad was going to stand in a Quiznos and work there. He decided to give me 25 percent of the Quiznos if I would do all the work. Chumlee came into play because he was already working in McDonald's and had that all-important fast-food experience. Our deal was that he would manage the Quiznos and work part-time at the pawn shop and quit McDonald's.

He had no problem with that.

Chumlee and I both went to Denver for Quiznos University. Some of the stuff they taught us could be applied to other business-related things, but since I grew up around businesspeople and knew the basics, I didn't really need to be taught basic math.

As great as my father can be in business, his biggest fault is that he can be impulsive. Normally, it takes two years to start a Quiznos. You scout out the location and do all the homework necessary to justify a quarter-of-a-million-dollar investment.

Well, my dad saw that a Quiznos went out of business on Fourth Street in Vegas. My dad says, "Hey, this one's close to the pawn shop." Obviously, not everything was perfect with the location since it went out of business. But my dad also saw they were building a giant courthouse/justice center right near it, so we figured we'd have no problem picking up a big lunchtime crowd from there. Even with Chum as manager.

Little did we know: They were building a huge food court inside the justice building.

Two years later, we sold the Quiznos to some other sucker.

FROM THE TIME I was in the third grade, the only thing I wanted to do was work in the pawn shop. If I had to write something in school about what I wanted to do when I grew up, I always wrote, "Work in the shop with Dad and Grandpa."

Funny thing, though: My dad and grandpa didn't share the same dream. My mom and dad didn't want me to work in the shop, not because they didn't think I could but because they thought I should decide upon a career path on my own.

I spent a lot of time in the shop, and that's what I wanted to do. Whenever I got suspended from school or sent home from school—which happened a lot—my dad would bring me into the store and make me sweep floors or clean the bathroom. There was no way he was going to let me stay home and watch television all day.

I needed a job after we got rid of the Quiznos, and I renewed my quest to start working at the shop. I figured if I hung around, he'd give in and put me on the payroll. Instead, my dad opened a business called paddletireking.com. He had been looking to buy paddle tires (big off-roading tires with tread that resembles paddles) for one of his all-terrain quads, and he couldn't find any online. So, my dad being my dad, he sensed a business opportunity and opened his own company. If he couldn't find what he was looking for, he figured there were a lot of people out there in the same position. Some people complain about it, some people start their own business to fill the gap. You could drop my dad off in the middle of Africa, and he'd find a way to make money.

"It's easy to do," he says. "Just apply yourself."

It helps when you have the vast amount of knowledge he has, and a fearlessness about taking a risk. Here's an example: One day my dad bought an original photograph off a guy who just wandered into the store needing some cash. The customer didn't know what he had, but he knew it was a reasonably valuable piece. My dad paid $1,000 for it, and when the guy left my dad said, "I think this could be a real steal."

It turns out the picture was taken by one of the few photographers whose printing plates are in the Smithsonian. Now, I know Ansel Adams and a few others, but I didn't know this guy. My dad did. Me? I still can't remember the guy's name.

The next thing you know, he's selling the photograph for forty grand. Remember, it's not our job to educate the customer on what he has—that's his job. The same as it's my job to know if something isn't valuable.

But if my dad didn't have his broad scope of knowledge, if he didn't spend four hours a night reading obscure books, he wouldn't have bought that piece. And it's more than just knowing; it's knowing *right now*, when that customer walks into the store with that photograph. The day-to-day workings of the shop don't always allow for him to call in an expert or step back into the office to do some research. If he hesitates, or if he's wrong, he can either miss out on a great opportunity or end up buying something that's worthless.

When it came to the paddletireking.com, my dad didn't have the time or the inclination to do the work (just like Quiznos), so he hired me to mount tires for $8 an hour. I worked out of a little room in the building across the parking lot from the pawn shop. The business was successful, and the work was hard. I was mounting twenty-five sets of tires a day, every day. In Las Vegas, in the summer, it was rough. Carrying around hot black tires in 113-degree weather—not fun. My dad was too cheap to buy a mounting machine, so he figured he'd hire the human mounting machine: me. I worked hard and kept at it, and most important I stayed out of trouble.

At about the time when I didn't think I could mount another tire, the night shift guy at the pawn shop quit. I talked to my dad about taking over that job, and he eventually gave me his best "Oh, what the hell" and moved me into the shop. And so began my progress through the ranks of Gold & Silver Pawn, starting with the shittiest job and moving up.

The night-shift guy works the walk-up window. The window is like a bank teller's window, with bulletproof glass and a slot to pass through money or items. It's the only part of the store that's open twenty-four hours.

And I've seen some stuff. You haven't really lived until you've seen a lady OD at the night window. Chumlee saw that once. Probably because once is all you need.

Chris Rock tells a joke about people at an ATM at three in the morning. His point is that anybody who's at the ATM at three in the morning is up to no good.

Well, I can do that one better: people at the night window of a pawn shop at three in the morning. Those are the people who have already sucked all their money out of the ATM. Either that or they aren't stable enough or together enough to even have a bank account to suck out of.

Either way, you see some things at the night window of a pawn shop in Las Vegas.

I'M SITTING ON THE stool inside the shop at the night window and a woman walks up and asks me, "Do you buy gold teeth?"

"Yes, ma'am, we do," I tell her.

She's looking at me through the window, and she doesn't look like a drug addict or a desperate person. She's in her fifties. She's dressed reasonably well, her hair is groomed, she's not dirty. (Those three descriptions qualify as high class for the night window.)

She says, "OK, good. Do you have a pair of pliers I can borrow?"

Stupid me, I think the two questions are unrelated. I think she's asking to borrow pliers for reasons that have nothing to do with the question of the gold teeth. I'm thinking maybe she needs to fix her car, or maybe give them to a guy she's with so he can fix the car.

It was late. I probably wasn't thinking straight.

I grabbed a pair of pliers from under the counter and told her I'd need a driver's license to hold so I make sure I get my pliers back. She nods and hands her license through the slot. No big deal to either of us.

About a half an hour later, she's still nowhere to be seen. I'm thinking it's awfully strange that someone gave up their driver's license for a pair of pliers at three in the morning in a pawn shop in Vegas. Then again, it is three in the morning in a pawn shop in Vegas, so maybe it's not so strange.

Anyway, she finally shows up at the window with her mouth full of toilet paper. She drops a gold tooth and the pliers through the slot.

A gold tooth covered in blood.

For $40.

So now I'm wishing I hadn't given her the pliers. If I had been thinking, I would have realized why she wanted the pliers. The idea wasn't to refuse the pliers out of any moral judgment—she's got to do what she's got to do. I just wouldn't have supplied her with the means to do that.

I'm looking at the tooth, thinking, "Well, Big Hoss—now you've *got* to buy it." After all, she did go to all that trouble to bring it to me.

I HAD A HOOKER come up to the window and try to sell me a Rolex. She slid it through the slot, and I took one look at it and slid it back.

"It's fake, I can't take it," I said.

Just then, out of nowhere, a guy in a purple suit—I kid you not, a purple suit—comes flying around the corner and starts beating her up. We have cameras trained on the night window, of course, and it was like this guy centered himself in the frame before he started hitting her.

Dude, you're on camera, buddy. Besides, I'm guessing it wasn't her fault the Rolex was fake.

I GOT REALLY GOOD at telling the difference between a real Rolex and a fake Rolex. If I hadn't, I might still be mounting tires.

But I wasn't always. The first week I worked the night window, I bought seven fake Rolexes.

Seven.

Even though my dad said he never wanted me to work in the shop, he was always teaching me about stuff. He's an enthusiastic guy, and he has all this knowledge stored up inside him. Sometimes he just has to air it out.

He had shown me Rolexes, and how to tell real from fake. They're a big part of our business. I was young and thought I knew a whole hell of a lot more than I did.

So. Seven fake Rolexes in a week.

To the tune of $25,000.

These weren't pawns, either—these were purchases. Evidently word spread in the fake-Rolex community of greater Las Vegas that a guy at Gold & Silver Pawn didn't know real from fake when it came to watches.

My ears still have the scars from hearing my dad and Old Man yell at me.

I thought for sure I was going to have to find another job. My dad was cool about it, though, and decided to chalk it up to a learning experience. When you see us on television, we're always a commercial break away from getting an expert onto the floor to examine something and tell us whether it's real and, if it is, what it's worth. That's TV, though, and there were no cameras rolling at 2 A.M. when I was buying fake Rolexes. I couldn't call a jewelry expert—or my dad—to show up and save the day.

The sad part is, I sat on my stool behind the bulletproof glass thinking I was robbing these guys blind. I was paying way less than I normally would for a new Rolex, and every time one of them walked away I chuckled to myself.

Turns out the joke was on me.

One of the tricky things about the business is the way people build their reputations within the shop. Some guys will offer everyone $5 for whatever they're selling, and it's inevitable you're going to end up with a few steals that way. There are too many desperate people walking through our doors, and a lot of them don't know what their items are worth. So if you low-ball everybody, there's a chance they're going to bite and you're going to look like a hero. That shouldn't be mistaken for knowing the business, though. It takes talent and skill to know the value of something. It also takes time and patience.

I learned that the hard way. But I learned. Now, if I happen to be burned by someone, I'll research and read to make sure I don't let it happen again.

THIS IS A CRAZY life even without a television show. I went a little nutty working the night shift. You can't make the mistake of thinking any of this—the city, the shop, the job—is normal. If you do, it can get inside your head.

The worst is when it's five in the morning and you've been up all night dealing with crazy, desperate people. Nights of big fights are the worst; it's like all the wild, crazy people in the world decide to descend on Vegas and turn it into a horror movie or something. On "normal" nights there's still a steady flow of people. The second you think you've got some time to stretch out and take a break, there are twenty people standing in line peering in at you with pleading eyes.

Charles is the longest-running employee we have. He's worked the night shift for fifteen years straight. He's a great employee, one of our best, and he deserves to be on the day shift. He deserves to be a manager. But all those years on the night shift have taken their toll. He spends twelve hours a night working by himself dealing with the night creatures. He gets jumpy. He can't function in the daytime when there is actual human interaction.

It's a different world outside that window. Once a guy came up in the middle of the night to sell his Skil saw. It was a busy night, probably ten people behind him in line, and he'd waited awhile to pawn his saw for a couple hundred bucks.

When he got to the front of the line, our night guy saw that the guard had been removed from the saw.

"I can't take it," he told him.

"Why not?"

"I can't sell it because it's not OSHA approved. It's worthless to us."

The guy argued. He didn't want to hear that.

"I'm going to pick it up when I get back on my feet. You're not going to have to sell it."

We can't operate that way, and the night guy told him so.

By this time, the people behind him in line were getting pissed off. They wanted him to leave so they could take care of their business. One guy was particularly loud. He told Saw Guy to get the hell out, to stop wasting everybody's time.

Saw Guy snapped. He turned around, raised his saw like he was going to throw it, and started pounding the guy's face with the blade. Over and over, he smashed that blade into the guy's face until it was a bloody, unrecognizable mess.

By the time the police and the ambulance came, Saw Guy had done enough damage to require five hundred stitches in the other guy's face. Our night guy said he couldn't get the image out of his head.

How are you going to stay normal when you repeatedly see that side of humanity?

ONE OF THE DUMBEST things you can do is sell a stolen item to a pawn shop. That doesn't mean people don't try it; it just means it's really stupid. Every item we buy or pawn goes into a database that gets downloaded to the Las Vegas Metropolitan Police every morning. Every item we buy or pawn is held for thirty days to give the police time to determine if it is stolen. The system is pretty airtight.

I probably write five thousand tickets a month—sale or pawn—and we might have six things put on hold. I've been subpoenaed more than two hundred times, but I've never once been called to testify in court. These guys always make a deal before it reaches that point; the case is rock solid once they get a signature on a pawn slip and the video from our surveillance cameras.

During the first season of the television show, a guy came into the shop to sell us a pair of diamond earrings. He agreed to do the negotiations on camera, and after the usual back-and-forth, we agreed to pay him twenty grand for the earrings.

On camera, we asked him why he was selling the earrings, and he said, "Oh, you know, I'm tired of having them, I need a little extra cash, this just seems like the right time."

We do the paperwork, file the transaction with the police department and Homeland Security, and the next day we get a call from Las Vegas Metro.

The earrings turned up hot.

I'm thinking, *Dude, you've got to be the world's dumbest criminal. You've got a camera in your face! You know they're stolen and you still did this?*

For an encore, I think that guy left our store and robbed a Dunkin' Donuts.

AS MY DAD ALWAYS says, "You never know what's going to come through that door." One day in 2007 a guy in his late twenties walked in and said he had a bunch of possessions to sell. I walked outside with him, and the first thing he wanted to discuss was an All American Chopper, beautiful and tricked-out.

"I paid seventy thousand dollars for this," he said.

We went back and forth, and I told him the most I could give him was eight grand. It was so personalized it was going to be a tough sell, and since my offer was so low I was surprised when he accepted it.

With that deal done, he started to move on to the next item. That's when I started to be a little concerned about him. He didn't look desperate or broke, but he was going about this operation so systematically that I started to think he might be selling everything as a prelude to suicide.

I was a little uncomfortable, so I asked him why he was selling everything.

"I'm heading back to Iraq in two weeks for my third tour with Blackwater," he said. "I'm going to party in Vegas for the next two weeks, because this time around I'm leaving with half the crew I had the last two tours. If I make it back, I'll have three hundred thousand dollars in my pocket to start over. If I don't, I won't need this stuff anyway."

So, yeah, my dad's right: You never know.

A LOT OF THINGS that happen in Vegas pass through our doors, in some form or another. It could be stuff, it could be people, but you could write a pretty good history of the city over the past twenty years through our store. We see celebrities, politicians, athletes. And we also see people who inhabit some of the seedier corners of the city.

During the summer months of 2007, I bought a couple of brand-new Rolexes from two different girls within a week. Both of them turned up hot, which meant I got burned for about twenty grand. The police tied it to an operation this guy—Arfat Fadel—was running out of Mandalay Bay.

It went like this: He hired girls to go into the spa lockers at Mandalay Bay to steal wallets and credit cards. Then he would send them to the Shops at Caesars to buy the watches, which a girl would bring to me to get fifty cents on the dollar.

We have no way of knowing these watches are hot—we get a lot of brand-new watches from people who can't get markers from the casinos and use their cards to buy expensive jewelry and watches to bring to us for their gambling money. It might not be the way you get your hands on cash, but some people don't have as many options.

So we're on to this guy. I'm pissed, because he burned me. The cops are pissed, because he's running a pretty sophisticated operation and they can't build a case because he's keeping his own hands clean.

Until about two months later, Arfat Fadel himself walks into the store, by himself. I recognized him from the police "wanted" posters. This time he's got an eighteen-carat Rolex Submariner.

I saw him from the time he walked through the door, and I'm trying to stay cool. He comes up and I greet him like everything's normal. (I hope.) He talks about the watch a little and then hands it to me.

I grab the watch and put it on my wrist and twist it around like I'm analyzing it. You know, look at it from one side and then the other, like I'm making sure it's the real thing. The whole time I'm trying to beat back the adrenaline that's pounding through my veins as I keep an eye on the bastard on the other side of the counter.

The idea was to walk around the counter, calmly, and proceed to beat the shit out of him until the cops got there and saved his ass. I got around the counter, but apparently I didn't hide my feelings as well as I could have. He started for the door the second I turned the corner, and I yelled after him, "I'm calling the cops to tell them you're selling stolen watches again."

I called Las Vegas Metro and told them, "I've got another stolen watch from your buddy in here. I'm holding it for thirty days."

They did a search and called me back: no report. He was in here selling his personal watch. Oh, well—he obviously didn't come back for it, so I at least got some of my money back from being burned on the other two.

Eight months later, on June 16, 2008, a wide receiver for the Oakland Raiders named Javon Walker was partying in Vegas when he made the mistake of getting into a Range Rover with a couple of guys who had been hanging out in the same clubs and casinos. Walker was drunk, and before long he found himself beat up—broken teeth, the whole works—and tossed into the parking lot of an abandoned condo complex a block off The Strip.

He was also missing about seventy-five grand in jewelry and several thousand in cash. The guy who beat him up and stole the jewelry—including diamond earrings that were yanked out of Walker's ears—was named Deshawn Thomas. The driver was Arfat Fadel.

If Fadel had stayed out of the thuggery business and stuck with the idea of stealing credit cards out of spa lockers at the Mandalay Bay, it might have been harder for the police to catch him. But he didn't. He went after an NFL player, and that's how the cops caught him. He ended up pleading out and getting a sentence of two to fifteen years. Thomas went to trial and was convicted, too.

That story made national news because Walker was an NFL player, but we knew Fadel before Walker did.

HERE'S A CUTE LITTLE story from the front lines of Gold & Silver Pawn:

Three of us were closing up the showroom one night around nine o'clock. There's usually a fifteen-minute period where we have to close completely in order to get the showroom shut down and open the window to let the night shift guy take over.

Two other employees, Brady and Travis, were closing up while this skinny little tweaker was at the window throwing a fit that we weren't helping him. He could see us in there, moving stuff around and taking stuff out of the cases to lock up for the night. He figured if we were in there, he should be our first priority. Well, he wasn't. We told him we'd get to him, but that didn't help.

He was out of control. "You fucking assholes, I need some help here!"

We told him to wait again, and he went down the line pointing at us—"Fuck you! Fuck you! Fuck you!"

We'd had enough. This guy was probably trying to pawn his Xbox games to get enough money to buy some more crank. It wasn't like he was going to make a difference in our bottom line. And since I quit, I have a hard time dealing with these guys. I probably should have more compassion, but I get disgusted by that drug.

Finally, Travis walks over to the window and says, "Screw you. We're not helping you. Go away."

The tweaker screams some more, but he does go away. We finish cleaning up and walk to the parking lot. It's the three of us and Old Man Dave, one of our security guys who is an ex-cop. Travis is walking toward his car, and out of nowhere the tweaker comes around a corner and gets in Travis's face. Travis spins on him and pushes him onto the ground, and that's when we notice the six or seven other guys popping up out of nowhere to take us on.

We've gone from telling this one guy to take a hike to fighting the entire Tweaker Nation.

I'm near my truck, so I open the door and get a ball-peen hammer out of the front seat. (I always carry a ball-peen hammer.) When I turn around, one of the tweakers is charging me so I smack him on the head with the hammer. By now my uncle who runs the tattoo shop across the parking lot is out there helping us out.

The whole time I'm waiting for Old Man Dave to end this. I know he's carrying a gun; it's part of his job to sit in the store and work security while armed. Instead, he's just beating on these guys—a sixty-something-year-old ex-cop just pounding these young guys. It took about thirty minutes for the police to get there, and by then the tweakers had scattered.

As we're standing there, I ask Old Man Dave about the gun.

"It was much more fun this way," he says.

We watched the surveillance video of that fight just about every day for the next two weeks. We had a great time with that. And the funniest thing was, a week after the fight Leftfield Pictures showed up to shoot the pilot for *Pawn Stars*. So a week before my big break as a television star, I was standing in the middle of a huge brawl in the parking lot.

PAWN STARS WAS ORIGINALLY supposed to feature me, my dad, and my grandpa. Then they dropped Chumlee into a couple of scenes and people just loved it. They were smart enough to include him as a main character, mostly as comic relief, and now his swag sells more than anybody else's. People come into the store looking for Chumlee T-shirts and shot glasses and baseball caps. What a crazy turn it's been for all of us.

Even a small slice of fame has its weird elements. I met my wife, Charlene, when we were in fourth grade. We were together from sixth grade through her junior year of high school, and then we took a five-year break in there. You can probably guess which five years those were, and what nasty habit I engaged in during the time.

A couple of years later, I finally got tired of hearing my mom say, "You really ought to find a nice girl like Charlene." So I asked her out, and we went out once and couldn't stand each other. About a year later, we went out again and a year later we were married.

Charlene didn't marry a guy on television, but she's been thrown into the craziness. Girls seek her out on Facebook and harass her about me. About *me*. That's when you know something is happening that (1) doesn't make sense; and (2) is a little bit creepy.

We were at a bar with some friends one night. Charlene was down the bar talking to her friends, and this girl came up to me. My wife walked over and said, "Hi, I'm Corey's wife." The girl started talking to her and asked, "Do you guys have any kids?" When my wife said we didn't, the girl said, "Well, then you're not *really* married."

So when I'm asked how my life has changed since the show, that's the kind of story that explains how crazy everything's gotten. I still don't think my life is all that interesting, but it's gotten quite a bit *more* interesting in the past couple of years.

A WORLD OF SECRETS

I'M ALWAYS TRYING TO PROVIDE HISTORI-
cal context on the television show. History is what I love, the
more unusual the better. And while I'm pretty conversant on
historical items such as Civil War muskets and presidential
signatures, I've also spent a lot of time studying and learning some
lesser-known facts.

In other words, I'm full of both useful and useless information.

I'll let you decide which category to place my extensive knowledge of
pimps and the history of their profession in. Fact is, I've dealt with a lot
of them over the years, and there are some interesting aspects of their
subculture, even beyond the crazy pimp rings we've had in the shop.

The stereotype of the pimp with the fancy, loud suit and the gaudy,
large jewelry is, in my experience, very true to life. But did you know
there's a practical business purpose for that jewelry?

Pimps buy a lot of jewelry from me, and the bigger the better. It's not
fake, either. They insist on real gold and they're willing to pay a good
amount for it.

And here's why: If they get arrested, the cops will confiscate their
cash but not their jewelry. They can give their jewelry to one of their

girls, and she'll take it directly to the pawn shop to get money for bail. It makes perfect sense if you look at it from their perspective.

The jewelry is not just an accessory for them, or a way to announce their success. (Or their profession.) They know that a pawn shop, as an industry standard, will give fifty cents on the dollar for jewelry that was purchased in that shop. And gold is always valuable to us, whether as is or as scrap. So to these guys, jewelry is economic security.

And when times get tough for the pimps, as they have since the economy went south, we see more and more of them sending their girls in to pawn the jewelry.

Hispanics are another group that has historically used jewelry as economic security. When you've been poor or beaten down or are skeptical of people's motives—maybe you distrust banks, or maybe you aren't in the country legally—you look for different avenues to provide security. If you're worried about being arrested or deported, and you don't completely understand what the police can and can't confiscate, you're going to rely on what you know. And a lot of people in that community have been taught about pawn shops.

There's something comforting in knowing you can buy a piece of jewelry from me and be guaranteed to get fifty cents on the dollar if you need to sell it back. They see it as wearing cash. Some bail bondsmen who cater to the Hispanic community will accept jewelry as collateral.

And if it makes you feel good to wear it, all the better.

These are the kinds of pawn-shop subplots that we don't get into on the television show. There's a backstory for just about everything. For example, on the show I ask nearly every customer, "OK, do you want to pawn it or sell it?" Almost without fail, the people who make it onto the show say, "I want to sell it."

There's a good reason for that, also: People don't want to be seen on television pawning their stuff. If close to six million people are watching you on television, you don't want that to be the image that beams out from the set. If someone agrees to be on television pawning an item, they have to agree to waive the confidentiality.

To sell something is a business transaction, but to pawn something is an admission. It's telling the world, *Hey, everybody—I'm broke.*

The people you see on the show are really selling their items. Most of the time, the rare and unusual stuff is more likely to be sold than pawned. We've got a reputation for dealing in that stuff—for being one of the few places outside of a museum or an auction house that does, in fact—so word has spread that we're the place to go. The show has made this more apparent, obviously, but even before, we'd get people coming through the door with someone weird saying, "My buddy told me you guys might be interested in this." Or "I don't know what to do with this, and I heard you might be able to help me out."

But in the real, everyday life of the pawn shop, people want to keep their stuff. So they pawn. There's something to be said for America's inherently positive outlook, because people who pawn fully expect to get their stuff back as soon as their life takes a turn for the better. They rationalize: *I'm just going through a rough patch right now; it'll be over soon and I'll have money to go back in there and reclaim my stuff.*

A guy who works for a living doesn't want to sell his tools. He wants to pawn them. He might wake up the next morning and discover the estimate he gave for that big kitchen remodel came through. So now he's got work, and he'll eventually have money, so things will be back to normal as soon as he can scare up the money to get into the shop and get his tools back.

And he's telling himself: *I'll never see the inside of a pawn shop again.* He might be right, and he might not be. If he's wrong, we'll still be there.

I see people who don't have *anything.* I see people who are *broken,* who don't have a dime to their names, a drop of gas in their tanks, or a scrap of food in their stomachs. They come to me and I have to tell them no. I can't help them because they have nothing to offer me. That sounds awful, but it's another stark truth of the business. More facts of life. Sometimes it'll just kill me—those people will just walk out the door and go sit in the parking lot to cry.

We'd had the television show for about a year when a marine walked into the store, and he was desperate. He was trying to sell me some piece-of-shit digital watch. It was the only thing he had of any value, and I had no interest in it.

He had the watch in one hand and a police report in the other. He'd had his wallet stolen. He'd lost everything, and he needed to get back to Camp Pendleton outside San Diego that day. He'd come to Vegas for the weekend, got robbed, and had no means of getting back. He was in a tough spot, to say the least.

"I can't take your watch," I told him. "I don't want to sound mean, but it's really worthless to me."

He was on the verge of tears. If he didn't find a way back—either by plane or bus—he was going to be declared AWOL. I was clearly his last resort, and he stood there, paralyzed, not knowing where to turn next.

"Wait here," I said. "I'll be right back."

I went into the back of the store, and I told everybody, "OK, here's what we're going to do: Everyone is going to give me twenty bucks, and we're going to get this guy back to Pendleton."

It wasn't a request, it was an order. I figured if everybody contributed, we'd all feel good about helping someone out. I passed the hat, and we rounded up enough for him to get on a bus in time to get back to the base.

It's a tough business. You see a lot of people you wish you could help, but if you start turning your business into a charity you'll find yourself right alongside those people. A pawnbroker with a really big heart isn't a pawnbroker for very long.

* * * *

EVERY ONCE IN A while we get the odd case of someone who pawns something for far less than it's worth and never picks it up. Perfect example: We had a guy come in and pawn a belt buckle that held two twenty-dollar gold pieces and a fifty-peso gold coin.

He used this buckle to borrow $50, and he did it on a regular basis. At the time, this buckle held about $1,200 worth of gold in it. You can argue about the sanity of wearing around a belt buckle worth that much money, but it was quite a sight. One morning, I went to the safe to see what items came off pawn that day, and there it was—the belt buckle.

And then there's the other cases: There's a Harley-Davidson shovelhead motor in the shop that's been there for fifteen years. This guy has been paying interest on his loan for this motor for fifteen years. We've made so much money off interest on this thing—he could have bought himself a brand-new bike with the money he's paid us in interest. But to him we're probably just a storage facility, and we can live with that.

It's not uncommon for people to use us for storage. If someone is going on vacation and doesn't trust their family members with a valuable piece of art or an antique, they can bring it in and have it under twenty-four-hour armed security for as long as they need. It's unconventional, but it makes some sense. When we sold non-antique guns, a lot of people would bring them in and pawn them while they went on vacation. They didn't want to leave the guns lying around the house, and we were an easy and safe alternative.

There are hundreds of items in the back room that have been there for *years*. It works out great for me—I'm happy to collect interest forever if they're willing to pay it—but it underscores one more great thing about my job: I don't always understand people. It's just a *thing*. Don't be so attached to it.

One of Corey's favorite lines in the pawn-shop business comes right after he's disappointed someone by refusing to give them what they want for something.

"Come on, dude," they say. "I've got good credit with you guys."

Corey looks at them and says, "Come on, brah, who you kidding here? People with good credit have credit *cards.* Just because you've picked up your shit a bunch of times doesn't mean I have to trust you."

I HAD A REGULAR customer who's a billionaire. An honest-to-goodness billionaire. He's a local guy, maybe late fifties, eccentric and cheap as hell. That's the key to his wealth: He never spends a penny.

For years, the sole purpose of my pawn shop for him was to get laid. I didn't encourage it, but that doesn't make it any less true: He used my shop to pick up chicks. Here's how his operation worked: Every two weeks or so he showed up with some young thing on his arm. We'd always talk; he's a fun guy, what am I going to say? He knew that I was in on his little game, and he was fine with that. He wandered the store for a while, showing her all the oddities before eventually making his way over to the jewelry counter.

He would then call me over to show her all kinds of expensive jewelry, and the girl would always go crazy imagining how it was going to look on her. Just as it reached the point where he either had to buy something or disappoint her, my billionaire friend would say, "OK, Rick, thank you very much. You can put it back in the case. We're going to go to my house and talk about it for a while first."

Never bought a thing. Two weeks later, he was back with a different girl.

Now, you ask: Why would he do this at a pawn shop? In Vegas, he could choose any of the high-end stores—Bulgari, Prada, Tiffany's—and probably impress the girls more than at Gold & Silver Pawn Shop.

Oh, but you'd be wrong, and here's why: Those shops wouldn't put up with him. Once, maybe twice, but after that he wouldn't be welcome in one of those places, no matter how much money he has. They'd get sick of him, and they'd be on to his game in no time.

Me? Hell, for me it's entertainment. I don't care what he's doing. I'm more concerned with good conversation with people who have lived interesting lives, and he fits that category.

I love to pick the brains of people who have expertise in unusual areas. Of course, I'm someone who can sit down and read a book on the history of batteries and be enthralled the entire time. (*The Battery: How Portable Power Sparked a Technological Revolution*—check it out.)

There's another rich customer who comes in because he has the world's largest collection of slot machines. Whenever someone comes in with an old slot machine, I'll call him up and see if he's interested. We'll go off on some conversational tangent that might take an hour, but in the end I've always learned something.

We have a group of little old ladies who have been regulars for more than a decade. They walk in every six weeks or so to see what's new. They want to see every single piece of jewelry, and they might spend an hour just browsing around. It's their outing, and I love talking to them. One of the downsides to the show is that I can't spend as much time talking to the old customers like them; there's just too much commotion when I walk out into the showroom.

I try to learn something from everybody. I try not to make moral judgments. Of course, in a pawn shop in Vegas, I wouldn't have too many customers if I was making a lot of moral judgments.

And that's how I end up learning things from the kinds of people respectable society would consider unsavory—like a pimp I'll call Calvin. Up until a few years ago, he came into the store regularly to buy jewelry or pawn stuff. There's an anaconda-skin suit in the back room—honest-to-goodness anaconda skin—thanks to him.

Calvin would roll up in the parking lot in the first of two tricked-out

Navigators. Riding with him were two of the most beautiful black women you have ever seen, along with four of the fattest, nastiest white girls. The second Navigator was filled with more nasty white girls.

I'm not trying to be mean here; I'm just telling the truth. These girls were not attractive in the least. But Calvin seemed to have an endless supply of them at his disposal, and finally my curiosity got the best of me.

"Calvin, don't take this the wrong way, but I've gotta ask you something."

"Shoot."

"How do you make any money with those white girls?"

Calvin nodded and ran a hand across his chin like a college professor getting ready to explain a complicated formula.

"Well, Rick," he began, "I'm going to let you in on some of the secrets of the secret society"—in his cadence, this is *see-cret so-seye-i-teee*. "A brother has been told his entire life that this"—he pointed to one of the white girls—"is the forbidden fruit. These two sisters here are absolutely beautiful, but if I bring any two of these others into the 'hood, I will make twice as much money."

Now, look—this guy's probably a douche bag. I'm not arguing that point. But I'll ask anybody anything, and sometimes that gets me in trouble. But more often than not, I'll ask my questions and come away knowing more than I did before I asked. I learned something from Calvin that day.

Calvin had tentacles all over the place. He worked in Vegas, and he worked in Arizona. He was working in Arizona when the cops finally caught up to him. They arrested him for pimping and pandering, and this time they had an airtight case. One factor they didn't consider: Calvin's cocaine habit.

He had a massive heart attack inside the county lockup. Once you're in police custody, the state has to pay for any medical issues that might arise, and they apparently weren't too excited about this down in Arizona.

As the story goes, they took him out of jail and dumped him at a nearby emergency room. He recovered and eventually made his way back to Las Vegas.

One day he walked back into the pawn shop. He must have just gotten back from Arizona, because he was down to nothing. He handed me a piece-of-shit gold chain that must have been the only thing of value he had left. I gave him twenty bucks for it, and as I handed over the bill, he winked and said, "You watch, Rick, I'm going to turn this into five grand by the end of the day." I don't know how he did it, but at the end of the day he walked back in with a pocketful of hundreds, got his chain back, and bought as much bling as he could.

People ask, "How can you stand it?" Stand it? I think the human race is the greatest thing ever! From my vantage point, every single day is a chance to talk to someone that most people would never have the chance to meet. It doesn't mean I have to live like they do.

After twenty-one years in the pawn business, I've learned that just about everybody is crazy in some way. Black, white, brown—all people have some aspect of them that's completely nuts.

This shop is a graduate-level class in human nature every single day. It's a wild, crazy, weird world out there, and I've gotten to meet just about every kind of wild, crazy, weird person who inhabits it. I have the greatest job in the world, because I get to see people in their native habitat. They don't sugarcoat anything with me—they lay it all out there.

Whenever I read a study conducted by a sociologist or someone who's trying to tap into the psyche of the poor or downtrodden, I picture the interviews in my head. Since I know the types of people they're talking to, I also know those people look upon sociologists or journalists as officials; people who are in some way connected to the system. They're going to tell them what they want to hear. Or at least what they *think* they want to hear. Either way it's different when they're talking to me with their guard down.

There are certain things you learn by working in a pawn shop that you might not get too many other places. For instance, I assumed everybody knew that strippers in higher-class clubs have to "tip in" at the beginning of every shift. We've had girls come into the shop for years pawning stuff to get their "tip in" money. It means this: It might cost a stripper $100 to go to work every night. As soon as she gets to work, she has to drop $100 in the tip-in jar to have the right to work that night. The club owners do this mainly because they can, but it also ensures the girls have an incentive to work hard to earn back the money. The tips they make for the night are theirs to keep, but they can't start work until they tip in.

I don't believe a sociologist conducting a study of low-income Americans would be told the story of "Father Unknown." Well, I've been told it more times than I can count. A large portion of poor people in this country write "Father Unknown" on their baby's birth certificate. They know exactly who the father is, but they put "Father Unknown" for a very practical reason: They get more welfare, and the government can't go after their boyfriends for the extra money. You put "Father Unknown" on your child's birth certificate, and it's a license to double-dip.

It all leads me to believe one thing: If you had a degree in sociology and came to work in my pawn shop for two hours, you'd throw it in the trash.

DIEGO CORRALES WAS ONE of the most entertaining boxers of his time. He was fearless, sometimes to his own detriment. He fought Floyd Mayweather Jr. in Vegas on January 20, 2001, for the WBC super-featherweight title. Floyd knocked him down five times, and Corrales got up every single time, ready to fight. After the fifth knockdown, his corner threw in the towel even though Corrales was screaming at them to allow him to keep fighting.

The Mayweather fight was seen as Corrales's coming-out party. He lost, but he gave an undefeated champion all he could handle. He fought him tough, and captured the imagination of the public when he was knocked down three times in one round and kept getting up.

As it turned out, though, he'd had better nights. And this one, strangely, ended up including us.

At the time he fought Mayweather, Corrales had vacated the IBF super featherweight title he had won the year before.

After the Mayweather fight—that very same night, as a matter of fact—he walked up to the night window and pawned his IBF belt for $500.

Remember, these guys don't get paid right away, and apparently Corrales wasn't in the mood to wait for his Mayweather money after this fight. He took the $500 and bought a shitload of cocaine. After some unknown amount of time, he went back to his house in Vegas and proceeded to get arrested for knocking around his pregnant wife, a move that ultimately cost him fourteen months in prison.

The belt was a conversation piece in the shop, but we didn't give Corrales a whole lot of thought afterward. Given his penchant for self-destruction, it was unlikely that we'd ever hear much from him after he got out of prison.

Wrong. He came out of prison and got right back to business. In 2005, he beat Jose Luis Castillo for the WBC lightweight title in the best fight of the year, by far. The tenth round was one of the most amazing rounds in boxing history. Castillo knocked Corrales down twice in the first minute. After the second knockdown, Corrales barely beat the count to get back up, and then he was penalized a point for spitting out his mouthpiece too many times. It didn't seem like there was any way he was going to win the fight, but he did. He drilled Castillo with a perfect right hand, stunned him, then got him against the ropes and pummeled him until the referee stopped the fight.

This guy was one tough dude, and crazy. Corrales and Castillo fought again, but Castillo weighed in too heavy for it to be a title fight. They fought anyway, and Castillo won. They were supposed to fight a third time—"The War to Settle the Score"—but this time Corrales weighed in too heavy and the fight was canceled.

On May 7, 2007, Corrales got drunk and went for a ride in Vegas on his Suzuki GSXR 1000—the fastest bike in the world. He misjudged the distance between him and the car in front of him while trying to pass and clipped the back of the car. They couldn't determine how fast he was going, but the only reason you have a bike like that is to go fast. He died at the scene.

I never wanted to sell his belt. This guy was a legend, and the story about how we got the belt in the first place was one of my favorites, the perfect Las Vegas story.

Unfortunately, someone in the shop didn't get the memo and sold it for just $1,500. That's one time when I tripled my money on a sale and wasn't happy about it.

GOLD & SILVER PAWN IS not in a good part of town. Nobody expects to find a pawn shop nestled among multimillion-dollar estates, but our neighbors are pretty shaky. There's a low-rent strip club/adult bookstore next door, and when I say "low-rent" I mean the kind of place you probably wouldn't want to walk into without wearing a hermetically sealed suit. (You'd throw it out as soon as you walked out, too.) We share a parking lot with the place, and the guys walking in and out of there are enough to make you question your faith in humanity.

Sometimes it's funny to see the tourists as they pull into the lot and look around before getting out of the rental car. They know the shop from *Pawn Stars* only and I know they're looking around thinking, *OK, I see the palm trees and the sign, so it must be the right place.* I'd love to hear the conversations as they decide whether they want to risk getting out.

They don't know the neighborhood used to be a lot worse. Across the street there's a relatively new government building, three stories and about a square block in size, which is about 20 percent occupied right now. When the housing boom was in full swing, they built this place to house the Building Department. Now that nobody is building anything in Las Vegas, there's no need to have the building. The most prominent parts of the building these days are the "For Rent" signs covering a lot of the windows.

Next to the government building is a parking lot for the employees. The lot used to be occupied by the infamous and ludicrous Normandy Motel. For years and years, the Normandy had a marquee outside that read, "Elvis Slept Here." That, apparently, was the only thing to recommend the place, and they kept using it long after anyone would have been excited to sleep in a building where The King once laid his head.

There might have been a time when the Normandy was a respectable place to stay on a trip to Vegas, but that time was before we moved in across the street. Come to think of it, there might never have been a time when the Normandy and "respectable" could be in the same sentence. For more than ten years, the Normandy was not only a dive, it was a whorehouse dive. The Normandy was a haven for skanky whores and crackheads and any other bottom-of-the-barrel types who found themselves on the wrong end of Las Vegas Boulevard.

The Normandy was also a source of entertainment for those of us working across the street. Our night window, which is essentially a bank-teller window, looked directly across to the front of the Normandy. It was our movie screen. While I was working at night, I saw girls run after guys buck naked down the street. There used to be a one-legged hooker who worked out of the Normandy. Some days she had a prosthetic leg, but on others she left the fake leg behind and got around with crutches. I saw a segment of society through that window that most people would like to pretend doesn't exist.

I know this sounds like a version of a guy-walks-into-a-bar joke, but

I swear it's true. One day a nun walked into the pawn shop to sell some Hummel figurines. She had a lot of them, so there was a lot of busywork going through them and deciding what kind of condition they were in and how much we'd pay for them. (This was one of the rare cases where I wanted to pay someone as much as possible, because I don't want to go to hell.)

I'm sitting in a stool behind the counter in the spot closest to the bank-teller window, which is on my right. The nun is across the counter from me, far enough away from the window that she can't see through it.

The whole time I was attempting to get through the Hummel figurines and get the nun her money, one of the guys I'm working with— he's sitting directly to my left—is kicking me in the shins trying to get me to look out the window.

I tried to shoo him away, but I could tell he was trying to stop from laughing. After six or seven kicks, I could feel a crowd gathering to my left. They were laughing and pointing. Finally, I couldn't help myself, so I stole a glance out the window and saw the cause of the commotion:

Two African-American hookers, completely naked, dancing on one of the Normandy's room balconies, in the middle of the day.

It was really hard to keep a straight face in dealing with the sweet little nun, I will tell you that. The juxtaposition of the nun and the hookers— let's just say it was surreal.

However strange it was, it is nowhere near the strangest scene involving the Normandy Motel and Gold & Silver Pawn Shop. That honor goes to an incident involving a man I'll call Donnie, who happened to be a regular customer of both establishments.

Donnie was a black man in his late twenties who had a great propensity for finding elderly white women who were interested in funding his fledgling rap career. He was a character, and his charms were such that he routinely came into the shop with a new elderly white woman and a new CD. It was always the one that was going to propel his career out of Las Vegas and into the hearts and minds of music fans worldwide.

It needs to be said that Donnie was a horrible rapper. I don't think much of rap in general, but his rapping was tragically bad. His songs had titles like "My Bottom Bitch" and other horrible things that make it even harder to believe he could recruit these elderly white women to fund his enterprise.

He was trying to look the part of the famous rapper, which is where we came in. Depending on the wealth of his lady friend of the moment, he was always coming in and either buying or pawning gaudy rapper jewelry. If it hung below the belly button or looked like it could be used as a lead for a horse, he bought it.

Back then, customers could still park on Las Vegas Boulevard, before the city added the palm trees. Anyway, Donnie pulled up late one night and parked in front of the shop on Las Vegas. He came to the night window and pawned some jewelry, and then he took the money back over to the Normandy for a night of fun and frolic with some of the working girls.

A few hours later, the night-shift guy was looking out the window and he saw Donnie coming back across Las Vegas Boulevard toward his car. About halfway across the street, Donnie dropped like a rock. Facedown— *boom!* Down goes Donnie.

Well, evidently Donnie did some drugs at the Normandy in addition to whatever else he was doing. The night-shift guy immediately called 911, and the emergency vehicles were there right away.

The next morning, the night-shift guy was all abuzz when we walked in to open up the store.

He told everyone, "Donnie dropped dead right in front of the shop last night. He was walking across the street and just went down. The paramedics came and worked on him for a while, then they put a sheet over his head and put him in the ambulance."

This was big news, because Donnie was the kind of customer every employee knew and every person who was ever in the shop at the same time would remember. The word spread: Donnie died. People wondered if he had family, or if there would be some kind of service where all the elderly white women who financed his stillborn rap career would come together to mourn him.

About three months later, I was working in the shop and a weird hush came over the store. It's hard to describe, but I was sitting at a desk behind the counter—next to Old Man—and it was obvious enough that I looked up. Everyone had stopped working and was staring at someone in the showroom.

I stood up to see . . .

. . . *Donnie?*

Donnie.

Guys were nudging each other like they were seeing a ghost. Donnie was walking up to the counter with a new elderly white woman. He was carrying another new CD that nobody would ever buy.

He was acting just like he always did, like he was on the brink of stardom and the rest of the world was just slow to catch on.

Nobody said anything to him. He was starting to look around at us like he was confused.

Since I'm the boss, I figured I better do the talking.

"Uh . . . Donnie?" I said.

"Yeah, Rick?"

"We thought you were dead."

"Oh, *that*?" he said, swiping his arm through the air toward the street.

"Yeah—*that*," I said.

"Oh, no. Just a bad night is all, man. Just a *bad* night."

THE LEGEND OF BIZZLE

HE HISTORY OF GOLD & SILVER PAWN wouldn't be complete without the story of Bill Urlaub, our most legendary customer. If we had a Hall of Fame, he'd be the first inductee, and the voting would be unanimous.

Bill was six-foot-seven and skinny as a garden hose. He wore shoes held together with duct tape and a set of dentures that he specifically had custom-made without lines. That's right: no lines. He looked like he was wearing a white mouthpiece. Whenever people saw him for the first time, you could see them staring at his mouth, trying to figure out what they were looking at.

Bill was in his late forties when we moved into our current location on Las Vegas Boulevard. Shortly after we opened as a full-fledged pawn shop in 1990, he started showing up every day. Often multiple times a day. At his peak, Bill averaged four visits a day.

And this went on for *years*.

Bill was a West Point guy, a retired firefighter, a retired school-teacher. These were his stories, anyway. He was in the West Point class of '65, and there's some debate as to whether he graduated. He admitted to shooting himself in the foot and receiving a Section 8 discharge for being mentally unfit for service. He was last in his class in 1965, and even someone with Bill's mental issues knew what that meant: a less-than-favorable assignment in Vietnam. Bill decided to get the shooting out of the way early, and on his terms.

He eventually became a firefighter, and he was let go from that job because of his psychological disability. Despite his obvious mental illness—his moods were contingent on his compliance with medical prescriptions from the first time he walked into the shop—he somehow got a job as a high school teacher, and he lost that job also.

What he was left with was a $300-a-month rental apartment in downtown Las Vegas ($400 with utilities) and $4,000 a month in various pensions or disability payments from the fire department and school district. He had no car and no other fixed expenses that we knew about. And just imagine where you're living if you're paying $300 a month for an apartment in boom-time Las Vegas. Hint: not a penthouse.

And yet, on the ninth day of every month—not the eighth, not the tenth—he would start pawning his stuff. He came in every day, but it was mostly to talk to us and hang around Old Man and generally make a pest of himself. We were nice to him and helped him out when we could; over time he became almost like the pawn-shop mascot.

Shortly after we opened the shop, when Bill was just getting to know everyone, he told Corey he would pay him $50 to deliver some carpet to his apartment. It was an easy $50, so Corey figured what the heck? When he got to Bill's apartment, Corey was amazed. Through him, Old Man and I got an idea of what Bill was spending his money on. Bill was *renting*, and yet he had crown molding on all the walls, fresh paint, a nice TV on the wall. He was decorating the place like it was the Ritz.

We also knew he gambled, but the money he gambled wouldn't account for blowing his entire monthly income in eight days. He must have lived hard-core during those days, though, because everything he picked up on the first was back in the shop on the ninth. And that was part of his deal: He couldn't live with himself if he didn't pick up all of his pawns when he got his money on the first. He thought we wouldn't like him anymore or something, because he had this compulsion for coming in on the first, walking up to the counter like he just won the lottery, and saying, "Well, I'm here to pay for my things."

Old Man loved Bill. If it wasn't for him allowing Bill to pawn his stuff, Bill probably would have struggled to eat. Old Man was the first one in the shop to make Bill feel like he was worth something, and he took pity on Bill and actually enjoyed his company, in small doses. Bill would talk Old Man's ear off, and Old Man would just nod politely or laugh. They went back and forth trading insults, with Old Man usually going easy on Bill by letting him get the last word.

One time they had a bet. I don't remember what the bet was—probably something Bill came up with and Old Man played along with—but I remember the stakes: If Old Man won, Bill couldn't pawn any of his crap in the shop for a month. If Bill won, Old Man had to take him out to a steak dinner.

Well, wouldn't you know it? Bill won. And Old Man—and my mom, for some reason—took Bill out to a fancy Vegas steakhouse. I think my dad was amused by the proposition until reality hit in the form of Bill ordering—and eating—three steaks before clearing everyone else's plate. I think it was the last time Old Man made a bet with Bill.

But Bill's capacity for placing a bet was legendary. Bill would bet on anything. And when I say anything, I mean literally *anything*. He hung out at Leroy's Sports Book in the Sahara, because Leroy's allowed betting on stuff that nobody but Bill would have any interest in betting on. He would come in and ask our advice on his bets, and he would try to convince us that we were really missing out if we didn't take *his* advice on bets. He always had a tip for us, and he always said it like it was inside information, like he knew some athlete—or a whole team—was on the take and the bet was a sure thing.

One day he walked into the store like he'd seen the rapture.

"Rick, did you know that Leroy's allows you to bet on Ukrainian professional volleyball?"

I said, "No, Bill, I didn't know that. *Why* would I know that?"

"Well, they do, and I'm thinking about betting on this one team. Here, let me show you why."

He proceeded to pull about five scraps of paper out of his pockets, all of them filled with his unintelligible scrawl. Apparently hidden within the scrawl were the secrets to betting success when it came to Ukrainian professional volleyball. To me, it looked like unintelligible scrawl.

After he was through, I asked, "Urlaub, how much are you going to bet on this?"

He looked up from his papers and said, "Five bucks."

HE CAME INTO THE store one day acting high as a kite, bouncing around talking to everybody. I watched him, thinking, *I don't think Bill took his meds this morning.* But as soon as he got close enough for me to understand the words that were firing out of his mouth like automatic gunfire, I discovered the source of his excitement: He'd won a superfecta on a horse race.

Winning a superfecta is a rare feat. It's when you pick the first, second, third, and fourth horses to finish in a race. Bill did it, and he was jacked.

"How much you win, Bill?" I asked.

"Oh, not that much," he said.

"Well, how much did you bet?"

"A nickel."

He hit a superfecta and he had a nickel on it.

Only Bill Urlaub.

His parsimonious gambling habits were a big reason why we could never figure out how he was always broke after the first eight days of every month. Gambling seemed to be his only vice, but he didn't bet enough for it to make a dent in his standard of living. Maybe from sheer volume, but not from the amounts he was betting.

Then again, this was a guy who had a bookie that allowed him to bet on *high school football* in Las Vegas.

Another time he came in and started bragging to Corey about having a hooker the night before. Corey wasn't that interested, but you didn't have to be interested for Bill to keep telling his stories.

Corey interrupted the story and asked, "Dude, how much you pay for a hooker?"

Bill says, "Four bucks."

We're almost on the ground laughing, trying not to let Bill think we're making fun of him. *Four dollars?* Corey says, "Dude, what kind of hooker do you get to come into your seedy-ass apartment for four bucks?"

Bill gets this little shit-eating grin on his face and says, "Corey, you know the difference between a four-dollar blow job and a hundred-dollar blow job?"

"No, I can't imagine."

"I'll tell you the difference: Ninety-six dollars."

The whole room broke up. The next time Bill came into the store, which was probably later that day, Corey shouted, "What up, Bizzle my Dizzle?"

This was during Snoop Dogg's heyday, and Bizzle stuck. Everybody who works here has a nickname, so why shouldn't our most famous customer? Besides, if you saw this guy with his mouthpiece teeth and his duct-taped shoes, the idea of calling him "Bizzle" was just too funny.

It stuck. From that point on, he was Bizzle. He even started calling himself that.

* * * *

I DON'T WANT TO make it sound like we made fun of Bizzle. We had our fun *with* him, but we also looked after him and took care of him. One of the ways we took care of him was by continuing to take his crap on pawn every month.

You might wonder: What kinds of things would a guy like Bizzle pawn when he showed up at the shop on the ninth of every month?

His two spare bicycle tubes, which were several years old and still in the box (pawned for $10).

His hammer ($10).

His Nevada state flag ($20).

His spare bike frame that he was always saying he was going to build up when he got enough money saved up ($20).

And, most famously, his weights ($25).

The weights were always the last item to be pawned, for obvious reasons. Bizzle didn't own a car, so he had to get his weights from his apartment downtown to the pawn shop, probably three miles, on his bicycle.

Picture this: a six-foot-seven man with duct-taped shoes and unlined dentures pedaling a bicycle down Las Vegas Boulevard balancing a forty-five-pound Olympic barbell with two forty-five-pound Olympic weights on the ends.

You haven't really lived until you've seen Bizzle rolling down the street with his weights. The man was a sight to behold.

OUR BIGGEST CHARITABLE MOVE toward Bizzle came when Big Hoss and Chumlee ran the Quiznos. They hired Bizzle to work in the store.

Yes, despite everything, they hired Bizzle. His loyalty would be unquestioned, that's for sure, and he'd do anything to make Corey happy.

He showered every day, so that wasn't an issue. We figured, what the hell?

Everything started fine. He might have been a little annoying, but the biggest complaint Corey had was about his eating habits. Every Quiznos employee is allowed one free sandwich for lunch. The first day the rules were outlined to him, Bizzle asked Corey, "What kind of sandwich are we allowed to have?"

"I don't know, Biz," Corey said. "Any kind you want."

At lunch that day, Corey watched in amazement as Bizzle went to work. He piled his high with turkey, ham, salami, three or four different kinds of cheeses. To top it off, he landed a big scoop of tuna.

As he was walking to a table to eat, he said to himself, "I think I'm going to need a knife and fork."

I bought the Quiznos to take advantage of its location across the street from the new federal building, but I failed to investigate well enough to learn about the food court they were building inside it. Regardless, Corey got a call one day from someone in a position of authority at the federal building. He wanted to open an account at our Quiznos so they could place large orders for meetings or conferences. This was big. Given the fact that Corey and Chumlee weren't exactly breaking records at Quiznos, this was *huge*.

Bizzle got caught up in the excitement. Corey and Chum were excited about it, so you know Bizzle was five times as excited. If it was big for Quiznos, it was big for Bizzle.

The day after the account was set up, Corey got an order from the federal building. It was big, too—probably $200 worth of sandwiches. Bizzle was, among other things, the short-distance delivery guy, so they sent him across the street with several bags of sandwiches. He didn't have to go far, he didn't have to collect money—it was foolproof.

About an hour after Bizzle left the store, Corey got a phone call.

Federal building.

"What the *fuck* is wrong with your delivery guy? We will never order from you guys again."

Corey is on the other end of this, thinking, *Oh, my God. What could he have possibly done? Was he even gone long enough to have done something so bad they're never going to order again?*

When the guy calmed down, he told Corey the story:

Bizzle was in a panic when he walked into the federal building to deliver the food. He practically ran up to the security guard at the front desk, handed him all the food, and yelled, "Where's the bathroom?"

It got worse.

Bizzle's trip to the restroom wasn't quite fast enough. No one knows whether he had trouble finding it, or whether it was crowded, or if he got hung up locking the stall door. Maybe it was something he ate, or the Vegas heat, or the excitement over the first of many big orders from the federal building. Whatever the case, the report Corey got from the folks on the scene was that Bizzle "shatter-blasted" the stall once he got in there. His insides exploded all over the walls, the floor—the guy even said the ceiling, but that might have just been hyperbole.

A few weeks later, Corey opened a piece of mail from the federal building. It was a bill, for $800 for cleaning the bathroom. The notation said, "Bio Crew."

And those folks at the federal building, give them this much: They kept their word. Corey and Chum's Quiznos never got another order from them.

BETWEEN THE FIRST AND ninth of the month, Bizzle came into the store four times a day to inform us why we should be betting Taiwanese racquetball, or high school football, or on what hole Tiger Woods would get his first birdie of a tournament. There was absolutely no end to the number of funky bets this man would make, and every time he was convinced he had unlocked the key to future wealth and happiness.

He was not shy about his opinions. He was gracious about sharing the inside information he had obtained through whatever means he obtained it. He was a regular at some of the less-expensive buffets around town, and he would often return to the shop after a hearty $1.99 lunch at the Nugget (fortified by the bag he brought back filled with pilfered food) telling tales of the important people he had guided toward the promise land.

"Saw the DA at lunch, Rick," he'd say.

"That right, Biz?"

"Oh, yeah, and he's gonna owe me *big*-time. I gave him a horse today that nobody knows about. He's gonna bet it, and it's gonna come up *big*."

Tuesday was his big day. Tuesdays were *huge*. Tuesdays were dubbed "T-Bone Tuesdays" in one of the downtown casinos, and like clockwork Bizzle would make his first appearance early on a Tuesday morning and proclaim to the shop, "It's T-Bone Tuesday. It's T-Bone Tuesday—four ninety-nine T-Bones on T-Bone Tuesday."

Without fail, he would make his way to T-Bone Tuesday, but he wouldn't go alone. Nope, he carried his trusty plastic bag, which he filled and brought home with him. Bizzle turned T-Bone Tuesday into something that could last all week.

As I mentioned, things changed some starting on the ninth day of the month. Tuesdays were still big, and it was still worth checking out the betting line on softball from Belize or some such place, but after the ninth, Bizzle's attitude had undergone a slight transformation. He'd pawned all his stuff, and he was out of money, so he figured he'd use the shop to make a little extra. His enthusiasm never waned, but its direction changed.

"Hey, guys," he'd say. "Anybody hungry? Need lunch? If you're too busy to get it yourself, I'll do it for you. Only a buck. Only a buck."

That was his post-ninth battle cry: Only a buck.

Need your car washed? Only a buck.

Need an errand run? Only a buck.

It got to be so incessant that we figured, what the hell? Give him a job to get him out of the shop and make him feel like he was accomplishing something. The money was secondary—we were already trying to take care of him without insulting him—so we figured we'd take him up on his offers.

He cleaned our cars. For a buck.

He'd clean the parking lot. For a buck.

He'd grab us lunch. For a buck.

The thing is, we would have paid him more, but that was his price and he felt he would be going back on his word if he took more than the quoted price. We learned early on that he wouldn't accept more, even if we presented it as a tip for a job well done. The price was a buck, and a buck it was.

Even if it was ridiculous.

There was one time I did feel bad about taking advantage of Bizzle's buck-an-errand policy. Every Thanksgiving, right after dinner, we pack up and head for the Glamas Sand Dunes, where we ride our quads in the dunes and have an absolute blast. We roll in about midnight, and one of our buddies has a DJ company, so within thirty minutes of us finding our campsite we have a full-on rager going. We leave everything behind and just have a ball, running our quads during the day and partying deep into the night. We do it with about two hundred thousand other people, which makes the late-night noise a little more acceptable. You don't go to Glamas over Thanksgiving weekend if you're looking for solitude and quiet.

It's also why our Thanksgiving dinner keeps moving up each year. Corey and I ask each other, "Do you think ten A.M. is too early to have Thanksgiving dinner?"

One year, about two days before Thanksgiving, Big Hoss was complaining about it being his turn to do the booze shopping for Glamas. He was whining like a little girl, saying he didn't feel like driving to the liquor store and why was it his turn and why can't someone else do it and why can't everyone just bring their own booze.

We've learned to ignore it, but still.

Well, Bizzle catches on to Corey's whining and figures we've got a problem and he's got a solution.

He'd do it.

For a buck.

Corey tells Bizzle it's a deal. Bizzle goes and retrieves his shopping cart from God-knows-where he keeps it. He comes back to the shop, thrilled to be needed, and asks Corey for the money and the list:

Fifteen 24-packs of Bud Lite
Four quarts of Jack Daniel's
Three quarts of Patrón

And on and on it went. Bizzle didn't blink. He folded the list, put it in his pocket along with the $600 Corey figured would cover it, and headed off to Speakeasy Liquor, located a half mile down Las Vegas Boulevard from the pawn shop.

About an hour later, here comes Bizzle, rolling a fully-loaded cart up to the front door of the pawn shop, bent forward like a guy pushing a car up a hill.

A half mile down with an empty cart.

A half mile back with a full cart.

For a buck.

He walked in, gave Corey some change and the receipt, and Corey handed him a buck.

You would have thought he won the lottery.

* * * *

I WISH BIZZLE'S STORY had a happier ending, but stories of guys like Bizzle rarely do, unfortunately.

Sometime in the first few months of 2009, Bizzle walked into the store all hyped up about some bet or another. He was talking a mile a minute, starting every other sentence with "No, really Rick . . ." and basically just being the same old Bizzle we'd known, loved, and tolerated all those years.

But something got into him that day, some impulse-control issue that probably happened more often than we saw. To us, he was eccentric and flat-out nuts, but he was never violent. He was one of the harmless mentally ill, people for whom there aren't nearly enough public services. He had no place to go, no friends to hang out with, so the pawn shop became his de facto home. And if it hadn't been for Old Man, who had a soft spot for the guy, he might have been dead long ago. Hey, some guys have bars. Bizzle had the pawn shop.

Well, on this day, as Bizzle was rattling on to Corey about some sure-thing bet, Peaches walked into the store to begin her shift. Peaches was one of our first female employees, not counting my mom and Tracy. As she walked past him on her way through the showroom, Bizzle reached out and slapped her on the ass.

Peaches was not happy, and she shouldn't have been. Corey was not happy, and he shouldn't have been.

Bizzle looked at Corey with a pleading look on his face, as if someone else had done the slapping. Once the shock wore off, Corey said, "Bizzle, you're done here."

He thought Bizzle was going to cry.

"Why?"

"Bizzle, if I let you in the store anymore, she's going to sue me for sexual harassment. You blew it. I'm sorry, but you're done."

And that was the last day Bizzle walked into the shop. Six months later, an acquaintance of his showed up at the shop—we don't know if he was family or what—and told us Bizzle had had a massive heart attack and died.

I honestly think being banned from the pawn shop broke his heart. When Bizzle got bounced from the pawn shop, he lost his home.

CHUMLEE

I GUESS I SHOULD START WITH THE NICK-
name. I wish I had a better story for how I got to be known
far and wide as Chumlee, but the truth will have to be enough.

My sister and I grew up with my dad in a blue-collar
neighborhood in Henderson, a suburb of Las Vegas. My dad raised us
pretty much on his own, and we spent a lot of time at the neighborhood
park across the street from our house.

When I was twelve, I made a new friend. It was a big deal for me to
find someone I could hang out with, since my sister and I were the
neighborhood punk-rock oddballs. Like me, my new buddy Tom was being raised by a single dad, and we hung out together at the park and at
each other's house.

One day we were at his house, playing video games in his room, and
it was getting to be around dinnertime. I figured I should probably leave,
so I headed downstairs to say good-bye to his dad and be on my way.

His dad was like my dad, working a lot and not around the house
very often. As I got to the bottom of the stairs, I could hear him in the
kitchen cooking dinner. On my way to the door I took a quick detour into
the kitchen to be polite.

"I'll see you later, Tony," I said. "Thanks for having me over."

He looked up from his cooking and said, "Where are you going? You ain't going anywhere until you sit down and have dinner with us, Chumlee."

I don't know what caused him to name me that, and at the time I had no idea what it meant. I was an outcast, even at twelve, with a new hairstyle just about every week. At this time, my hair was crazy even by my standards: It was cut to look like a monk's, with the crown of my head shaved and a ring of hair starting about an inch above my ears. No monk would do what I did to top it off, though. The ring of hair on top was spiked, colored orange and red, and every four inches or so was tied with a rubber band. It looked like the Statue of Liberty crown.

It was designed to shock. I thought it was cool.

From the moment the word "Chumlee"—is that even a word?—left Tony's mouth, I was cool with the nickname. I thought, *Chumlee—I think I'm going to roll with this.* Maybe I was flattered that someone thought enough of me to give me a nickname, I don't know, but I liked it even though I had never heard of the Tennessee Tuxedo cartoon or Chumlee the walrus. And once my friend's dad told me why he named me that— my body reminded him of a walrus's, I guess—I was still cool with it. I wasn't insulted. I've always been pretty easygoing.

And I guess because I was cool with it, the nickname stuck. My real name is Austin Russell, but there are maybe twenty people in the world who call me by my given name. People in my family or people who went to elementary school with me and knew me before I was twelve call me either Ozzie, Austin, or Oz. To the rest of the world: Chum, Chummie, Chumster, Chum-Chum to little kids, and Chumlee to anybody who's ever watched the television show. It's the all-purpose nickname with a hundred variations.

* * * *

MY CHILDHOOD PROBABLY WASN'T ideal, but it never felt anything but normal to me. My mom wasn't around much, and my dad worked for himself, so my sister and I had to fend for ourselves most of the time. She's a year younger than me, and we pretty much made our own way—and our own rules. We didn't think we were underprivileged or at-risk, but I'm sure it looked different from the outside.

My dad was a master carpenter, but there were times when he struggled to get food on the table and pay the bills. We usually had food, and clothes on our back, but there wasn't always a lot of food and the clothes were rarely new. Dad was the president of his chapter of Alcoholics Anonymous, and that took a lot of his time, too. I think his work with AA was his true calling, and if he could have done that full-time and been paid enough to keep us going, he would have gladly quit the carpentry work. Some of my strongest childhood memories center on cigarette smoke: My dad always had a bunch of people sitting in the living room and at the kitchen table, telling their stories and smoking like mad. I've never smoked cigarettes, but my lungs probably look like I have. There was a permanent cloud of smoke in my house throughout my childhood, or at least that's the way I remember it.

Here's the signature story from my youth: I was in ninth grade, and one day it was more important for me to go and help my dad finish a job so he could get the bills paid than it was for me to take my final exams. That's a true story. Instead of taking my final exams, I went and helped my dad. He paid me for my time, but it was just understood that I was needed more with him than I was in school.

I never felt I had a hard life. I never had resentment. When I became a teenager, my dad said to me and my sister, "I raised you guys to know the difference between right and wrong, and from here on out you're going to have to make your own decisions. I'd rather have you guys mess up on your own and learn as you go than have me decide your life for you and you don't make those mistakes until you're twenty-five."

There were many times when we had to rely on the kindness of others to make it. We got a lot of government food—frozen pizzas, butter, all kinds of weird and not especially healthy stuff. I don't know how it happened, but one time we had close to a hundred one-pound sticks of butter in the refrigerator. Anyone who came over and opened our refrigerator would go, "Whoa—what's with all the butter?" We didn't have to buy butter for about two years.

When I was thirteen, my dad got married and they had a son, my half brother. My sister and I helped raise him for the first five years of his life, until his mother decided to stick around. (Biological moms who don't always stick around seem to be a theme with Corey and me.) It's crazy to think I was raising a newborn baby when I was thirteen, but that's the truth. My sister was twelve, and she was right there with me. I think we did a pretty good job.

My sister and I were close. We had to stick together; all we had was each other. As the older brother, I had a protective bond with my sister, and that's how I got to know Big Hoss. Our relationship had a rough start. He and my sister were in the same class—fifth grade—and I was in sixth. She came home one day and told me Corey was picking on her.

This wasn't cool. Nobody picked on my sister without dealing with me. I went over to the park near my house and waited for him. I knew he would show up there—all of the neighborhood kids hung out there—and sure enough, he came barreling down the hill on his Rollerblades. I jumped out and tackled him onto the grass. He was a big boy then, too, so it was probably a pretty good collision. We grappled for a minute, just flopping around, and then he left.

He wasn't done. Two weeks later, he came back looking for revenge. You know how it is when you're a kid in a blue-collar neighborhood—you can't lose face. You can't have everybody at school saying that a guy that looked like me got the best of you. This was probably a big deal back then, but it seems pretty silly now. He knew he could find me in the park, because I could be found there every day with my skateboard. When he came back, he walked up to me and pushed me in the chest, and I pushed him back, and before long we were in the most pathetic fight ever, just a couple of idiots flailing their arms and rolling over on each other. After a few minutes of this, Corey choked me out and was declared the winner of the big fight.

Afterward, we sat on the ground talking shit to each other. It was really stupid.

After that, we kind of left each other alone, but one day after school he got into a fight and he was getting beat up pretty badly. I stepped in with a couple of other guys and broke it up, and he looked at me with a look that said he was surprised but thankful that I did it. We realized then that all of our friends were friends with each other, and that it was probably really stupid for us to keep up this fake feud. Once we realized we really weren't as different as we thought we were, despite my punk-rock persona, we knew it made more sense for us to be friends than enemies. Being enemies took a lot more work, that's for sure, and I wasn't interested in flopping around on the grass in the park trying to keep Big Hoss from choking me out.

So from those humble beginnings, we started hanging out and became best friends. This friendship happened even though Corey's parents didn't want him hanging out with me. My sister and I were the wild punk-rock kids with crazy hair, the outcasts. Everybody knew us, and we didn't fit in with the crowd. I had my tongue pierced in seventh grade, and we were coloring our hair way before anyone else in the neighborhood was. Rick and Tracy looked at me and thought the worst thing for Corey would be to hang out with me.

"We don't want you hanging around with Chumlee," Rick would tell Corey. When Corey would ask why, Rick would say, "Uh . . . just *look* at him."

They didn't know my house was really different than it looked. My dad's work with AA meant we had people in our house all the time, and they kept an eye on us. Sometimes there were people around the house even when he wasn't. It was a different upbringing from what you see on television sitcoms, I guess, but when you don't know anything else, you just accept it for what it is. Just life, you know? My dad grounded me only for ditching school. That, he didn't like. But with most other things, as long as it didn't involve getting arrested, I was left to make my own decisions and mistakes.

It took Rick and Tracy a long time to realize that *Corey* was the bad influence, not me. I was the calm one, the one who usually wanted to do the right thing. I have to admit that I wasn't an angel, but Corey had a much stronger wild streak than I did. We both goofed around with drugs and partied the way you'd expect of kids with too much time to themselves, but I was always the one who knew when to stop. Corey? Let's just say it took him longer to learn his limits.

At some point, Rick and Tracy got hip to the idea that Corey's behavior was not being influenced by me. When that happened, their opinion of me underwent a massive change. I went from being the bad influence to being the good influence, and I could do no wrong. I didn't deserve it, but I didn't argue. I was the Teflon man, and I have to admit it felt good.

When we went to Reno for Job Corps, I wrecked Corey's car. I was trying to learn how to drive, and I hit another car. To this day, his mom thinks Corey wrecked it and I just took the blame to keep him out of trouble.

I told her, "I hit the car. I was just learning how to drive and I screwed up."

Tracy said, "No, no, Chumlee—I know you're just doing this for Corey."

No matter what I said, I couldn't change her mind. After a while, I just stopped trying. I'm not so stupid that I can't see a good deal when I get one.

✳✳✳✳

WHEN COREY WENT TO Reno for Job Corps, I was working at Wendy's and living my life without a whole lot of direction. I had worked at Burger King and I would go on to work at McDonald's—as an assistant manager, I'll have you know—so I became kind of an expert in fast-food employment. If you asked me to give you a scouting report, I'd say McDonald's had the most serious environment. Wendy's is the place to work if you want to flip burgers at your buddies who are working the counter and generally goof off. I don't know too much about Burger King because I didn't work there long enough to even figure out that whole flame-broiled thing.

I hung out with the Harrisons a lot when I was a teenager. When I was sixteen, I showed up at their house on Thanksgiving because there wasn't enough food at my house. I ended up spending a lot of holidays with them, and when Corey was in Reno I would go over there and hang out with Adam. I also liked the food.

Corey had been in Reno for about three months when Rick had a little heart-to-heart with me at his house. He was sending Adam to Job Corps, too, and he told me I'd be better off learning a trade than flipping burgers across the room at Wendy's. Rick's smarter than me, so I figured he was right. The next day I went down and filled out the application.

A lot of good things happened for me in Reno. I was taught how to be an electrician, and you could start a good argument by asking Rick who was the worse electrician: me or Corey. Neither of us ever collected a paycheck as an electrician, but that doesn't mean Job Corps was a waste of time. The program was great, but it was where probation officers from Los Angeles send a lot of their clients, so there were guys like me and Corey mixed in with a bunch of gangbangers from L.A. Out of the classroom we had too much freedom, and with a few hundred guys and girls living in dorms without much supervision, it got to be a free-for-all sometimes.

I stayed in Reno to get my high school diploma. I'm not proud of this, but I paid people $25 per test to take three of my equivalency exams. That was kind of the atmosphere at Job Corps: anything goes.

When we got back, Corey and I got an apartment together. This is when the partying went into high gear. This is when I started doing a lot of meth with Corey, and we set about the task of pretty much wasting our lives. We hadn't lived together very long when Corey got a collapsed lung and Rick had to come over to help him. Rick hadn't been to our apartment yet, and when he pulled up in front of the complex he didn't even have to call us and ask which apartment was ours. He just walked up to the one with the most garbage in front of it and knocked on the door.

He was right. Isn't that pathetic?

I got to the point where I couldn't do it anymore. Our pattern for about three months was to stay awake for four or five days at a time and accomplish absolutely nothing while we were awake. I was sitting there on a couch one day holding a pipe in my hand, thinking, *What am I doing? This isn't me.*

The way we were going, and the way our friends' lives were going, we both knew either death or prison was in our near future. I only got involved in meth for a short amount of time, but it dug its claws into me so fast and so hard it scared the shit out of me.

Corey was still partying and I said, "Corey, I just can't do this anymore."

We decided to pay our last month's rent and part ways. It was tough, but we had to fix ourselves. This happened during the summer before my little brother started kindergarten, so I moved back into my dad's house to help him with my brother. He needed someone to take my brother to school in the morning and pick him up in the afternoon because my sister had just gotten married and moved to Utah. It gave me a good reason to refocus and get my life back together.

My dad never preached recovery to me. He knew what I was doing, but he stayed consistent with the way he raised me. He let me make my own mistakes, and he let me figure out the solutions.

I've been around recovery my whole life. I didn't think I was addicted to meth; it was a three-month thing that I regretted even while I was doing it. But I thought about those people at my kitchen table telling their sob stories just about every night. My sister and I went to AA meetings with my dad because there was nowhere else for us to be. Even though my dad never threw it back at me, it was ingrained in me.

We listened to all of it. *Keep coming back. It works if you work it.* Saying their prayers and shaking their hands.

For the better part of two years, that was my life: taking my brother to school in the morning and picking him up in the afternoon. About this time, Corey's life spiraled out of control. He hit bottom when he ended up in jail after a bad trip had him thinking some girls had stolen his dad's car. When he moved to California to live with his mom, we fell out of contact for a while.

I kept helping my dad with my little brother while I worked as an assistant manager at McDonald's, completing my fast-food trifecta. I stayed away from meth and felt like helping raise my brother gave me a purpose in life. I learned some responsibility at McDonald's because I had a good manager who taught me how to handle myself. It wasn't the perfect life, but I was a productive member of society.

When Corey got back from California, he called me up to see if I was still clean. He didn't want to associate with any of the guys from our past who were still using because he'd worked so hard to kick the drugs that he didn't want to be around anybody who might tempt him to go back to his old ways. Once I stopped, I never gave it a second thought except to kick myself for ever starting in the first place.

Corey started coming by the McDonald's three or four times a week and we'd hang out. I don't know if it was my dad's influence or what, but I felt a responsibility to help Corey stay clean. It gave me another purpose in life, and since I knew how easy it could be to slide back into the old lifestyle, I made sure Corey was never in a position where he might make the wrong decision.

When Rick bought the Quiznos and gave Corey a percentage for his birthday, Corey told me I needed to quit working at McDonald's and help manage the Quiznos. I figured it was a good chance for me to get some more management experience, plus it allowed me to add to my fast-food résumé. That was an important factor in my decision.

There were a lot of things that went wrong during our reign at Quiznos, but most of it boils down to this: I didn't manage the place properly. You know, I wasn't ready for that kind of responsibility. I never took inventory. I just faked it. Quiznos's corporate policy demands that you fill out these forms every morning, and I was always at least ten days late. And they were probably never right. I didn't give a shit because I was twenty-two and stupid. I wasn't ready to manage a business.

Somehow, Rick gave me a second chance. I still enjoyed my second job at the shop, and Rick gave me a second chance by making me full-time. I loved it from the first day, even with Old Man constantly teasing me. Nobody ever thought it would lead to us being in a television show, and being kind of famous, and having such a great time. I never knew what the word "surreal" meant before now, but this is surreal.

I was working the night shift for a year before the show started, and they switched me to days about a month before they started filming. The night window is another book entirely. One night I'm sitting there minding my own business when all of a sudden *boom!*—a four-hundred-pound woman falls into the window. She got up and *boom!*—there she was again.

"Help me!" There was no one in line and she was out there by herself screaming.

I said, "Ma'am, I can't call the ambulance until you tell me what's wrong. Tell me what's wrong."

"Help me!"

The night window is home to a steady stream of crazy people. They appear at all hours, in all conditions. I didn't know what was wrong with this woman, and I didn't want to call the ambulance if she was pulling a scam or trying to get me to come out of the store so ten guys with shotguns could come around the corner and storm the place.

I was trying to figure out what was wrong with her, but she still wouldn't tell me. She passed out under the window, and I opened the little teller's window and splashed a Dixie cup of water on her. She woke up and I asked, "Ma'am, are you all right?"

"Call the ambulance."

"I can't call an ambulance unless you tell me what's wrong. If you scoot up to the curb I'm sure one will come by and pick you up. They come by all the time."

She scooted to the curb, and within five minutes an ambulance stopped. As soon as they got to her, she said, "I'm ODing on heroin."

All she had to do was tell me that and I would have called for her. It's not like I would have held it against her. After all, I was working the night window in a pawn shop. I'd seen everything.

IT'S KIND OF A fluke that I ended up on *Pawn Stars*. I know everybody who watches me on television probably says, "Yeah, you look like a fluke," but I'm talking about a real quirk of fate. If I had stayed on the night shift, I wouldn't have been on the show.

Leftfield Pictures was developing the show with three characters—Old Man, Rick, and Big Hoss. There were only about ten other employees in the shop at the time, so we were always hanging out and watching what was going on.

They tried out a few other employees, including me, as they were going along. During the scenes they filmed with me, I think they liked the chemistry between me and Old Man. These guys know they can say whatever they want to me and I'm fine with it because they love me and I love them. And since Old Man says whatever's on his mind, it worked out pretty well.

If you came into the shop and heard the banter back and forth, you might say it's a hostile work environment. Come to think of it, it *is* a hostile work environment. Most people probably don't want to be put down all day, but we just throw words around and everybody can take it.

I'm referred to as the village idiot—Corey coined that term during the pilot. They needed some way to explain who I was, since everyone else was family. Corey said, "This is Chumlee. He's my childhood friend."

He kind of paused, thinking of what he should say next.

"He's . . . uh, what we refer to as our village idiot. Every village has one."

I admit it: I'm not very book smart. But if you put me on the street I'll make it every time. I don't read a lot. I don't spell very good at all. I don't know where periods and commas go. But if you put me on the street with nothing, I'll make something up. I'm very wise and street smart and I have common sense. I'll take common sense over book smarts any day where I come from.

We've always been hustling—gold, T-shirts, whatever. Corey's been buying little chipped diamonds from people since he was twelve years old. We've always had a little hustle going. It's kind of where we're from, and this place puts it into you.

Corey is really smart, like Rick. He has all the street smarts and he's smart with books. People don't give Corey enough credit for being smart because he comes across as a hard-ass on the show. He is a hard-ass, but he's really intelligent and earned everything he had. That's a big misconception about Corey; he didn't grow up with a silver spoon. His dad never gave him anything—he had to work the night shift for a year when he first got here.

You could say my life has changed a little bit. I'm living in a nice place and trying to figure out how I can put my money away to make it last as long as possible. That's a lot different from where I was fifteen, or even five, years ago.

The only regret I have is that my dad died about a week before the first show aired. He knew it was happening, and he was proud of me, but he died in Georgia before he could see me on television. He suffered from pancreatitis and ultimately died of pancreatic cancer.

My dad was sober for the last twenty-five years of his life, but it was still the drinking that killed him. All the medical problems he had were because of the long years of drinking before he stopped. It didn't seem fair to me that he devoted so much effort to his own sobriety—and that of others—and the drinking still got him in the end. It hung with him like a cloud.

I carry my dad's memory with me. I might not have had the most conventional childhood, but he did the best he could and taught me a lot of good lessons. He always told me, "If you don't have the money to buy it, you don't need it." He never used a credit card or bought anything unless he had the cash. We didn't have much, but he put away a few dollars at a time and eventually bought a big-screen TV.

When he sold his house in Vegas and moved to the hills of Georgia, I kept tabs on my brother from a distance. Then after the show hit it big and I got some extra money, I brought him out for the summer. I send him school clothes and school supplies whenever he needs them.

Everybody knows I'm crazy for sneakers. I can tell you the history of every Nike shoe and the designers who designed them. I'm smart about weird stuff. Rick calls me an "idiot savant" when it comes to shoes, but he likes them, too. My little brother has got to be the only middle-schooler in the hills of Georgia who has first-edition Nike custom shoes and a Gucci backpack.

✳ ✳ ✳ ✳

I HAVE NO PROBLEM with my character on the show. They can call me a village idiot or an idiot savant or any other kind of idiot they can think of. Hell, I sell three thousand T-shirts a month. I can put up with a lot of words for that.

We have a friendly competition in the shop when it comes to the swag sales. I usually win. I started out thinking I could handle all my own T-shirt sales, and I developed my own shirt—it's white with a depiction of me in a Roman helmet, like a centurion—and sold it through my website.

I had it delivered to the store and I had to handle all the orders and all the shipping. I was getting good money, but it was a lot of work. Rick saw it and wanted to buy half the company for $5,000, and I told him no. I wanted to do something on my own, and this seemed like something I could handle. So I did, for about six months, before the hassle got to be too much.

I was spending two hours a day sending out T-shirts, and the more I thought about it, the more I realized it would be a lot easier to let Rick handle it along with all the other stuff he was selling through the shop. They had a system going, and it was way more efficient than mine. I might get twenty cents less per shirt under this deal, but someone else puts it on the shelf and sends it out.

HERE'S SOMETHING NOBODY WOULD believe about me: I'm a pretty good basketball player. Seriously. If you doubt it, you can always ask Big Hoss.

Because you know what? Big Hoss learned the hard way.

About six years ago we were hanging around my apartment and Corey saw a basketball sitting there. He said, "You're no good at basketball. What are you doing with this?"

"I'm hella good at basketball," I said.

He didn't believe me. He didn't know I'd been hanging out at the park playing basketball just about every chance I got. He kept acting like he didn't believe me, so I said, "OK. We'll go to the park right now and I'll bet you a thousand dollars I can beat you in a game to twenty-one."

Before he could respond, I said, "And I'll give you eighteen points."

That got his attention. All he needed to do was score three before I scored twenty-one. How easy is that? He picked up the ball and said, "Let's go."

It took me about six minutes to beat him. He'll tell you I scored twenty-one straight, but that's not true. He quit before I could get to twenty-one. I scored twelve or thirteen in a row and he just walked off.

I got moves. I got crossover moves, I can bust the three. I haven't played much in a while, but back when I was playing, I was way better than you would expect. Corey couldn't hang with me, I know that for a fact.

OH, AND ABOUT TWO years after Corey and I got to be best friends, we were talking about why I jumped him that day at the park.

I said, "You were picking on my sister, and I needed to stick up for her."

He said, "What? I wasn't picking on your sister. I was picking on your neighbor."

You mean all that fighting was based on a misunderstanding? Man, I wished I'd known that. It would have saved me a lot of flopping and flailing.

13

EASY MONEY

THERE'S NOTHING BETTER IN THIS world than an irrational consumer craze. Nobody knows how they start, or how long they're going to last, but they can be the greatest thing that ever happened to a guy like me. I'm always searching for ways to make money, but an irrational consumer craze comes to *me*. Give me a good fad—the more ridiculously senseless the better—and I'll be happy as hell until the next one comes along.

The average American consumer, the one that shops at the mall and wants the best for his kids and watches a lot of television, is influenced by popular opinion. If there's something out there that goes from being a product to being a fad, he's there. If his kid wants it, he'll do anything for it. If there's a chance he can make a buck off it, he'll go after it. For me, any irrational craze is money in the bank.

I got my first taste of it when I jumped into the designer-jeans fad of the late 1970s. I was fourteen years old, still living in San Diego, completely uninterested in school and completely interested in making money. The jeans that fueled the craze were Jordache jeans. This company had been making jeans for a while, but it took a huge marketing push to turn their pants from niche product to national fad.

My mom and I were doing a lot of things around this time, trying to make some extra money. She found knockoff Jordache jeans in Los Angeles, and she bought a bunch of them for us to sell at the weekend swap meets. We were doubling our money by selling these jeans to kids who either didn't know—or didn't care about—the difference between real and knockoff, or couldn't afford the real thing so they were happy to have knockoff Jordache jeans. I was making two grand a week off these things.

I didn't know it then, but I was capitalizing for the first time on the irrationality of consumers and the economy's ability to create a secondary market that was ripe for profit. It's like identifying one market and creating another to satisfy it. And my first trip into the underground economy was a profitable one.

After we moved to Las Vegas when I was sixteen, we were always looking out for a quick way to make money. Before, when my mom's real estate business was active, we did it to make some extra money and to do something we enjoyed doing. Now, with my dad's small coin store struggling to get a foothold, we were doing it for survival. We went from hustling as a hobby to hustling as a way of life.

And I can tell you one thing without fear of contradiction: Nothing gets Old Man more excited than frenzied people throwing money at him over inexpensive stuff.

Which brings up another great thing about Las Vegas: If it's going to hit, it's going to come through here. With the number of people traveling here from other places, and the consumerism of a casino-based economy, Vegas is the perfect place to make a few bucks identifying and exploiting a quick fad.

My first Vegas-style success? Gucci bags. When I was sixteen, Gucci bags were big. Real big. Gucci came into the U.S. market with a bang, and Gucci handbags were the company's first big item to tap into the irrational nature of the consumer. I was always combing secondhand stores and estate sales, and one day I walked into a store in a nondescript strip mall across from the MGM Grand and found knockoff Gucci bags for $10 apiece.

Remember: At this time, roughly 1981, every girl between the ages of twelve and twenty-five would do anything for a Gucci bag. And girls that age weren't too hung up on whether the bag was a knockoff, because their friends probably didn't know the difference or didn't care either way.

And right then, standing in the store across from the MGM, I'm looking at $10 Gucci bags that, if real, would sell for $300. I consulted my mom, asking her to come down to the store with me to assess which ones would sell the best. We got together and bought sixty Gucci bags for $600, went to the swap meet that Saturday, and sold every damned one of them for $30 each. Tripled our money.

For the next four months, Gucci bags ruled our lives. All we did was buy and sell these $10 Gucci bags for $30. Made a ton of money for a sixteen-year-old kid. Then one day we packed all our Gucci bags in the trunk and headed to the swap meet, only to find about four or five Asian people selling Gucci bags for less than we were buying them. And that's how we discovered the bottom had fallen out of the knockoff Gucci bag market.

Our store gave us an anchor, a place to sell the hard-to-get items that people wanted. But we still went to the swap meets and sold stuff there. It helped us sell a lot of things at once, but it also gave us the opportunity to observe and listen to people as they shopped. We got ideas by listening to what they perceived to be hot items, and we were able to see what other people in our position were selling, and for how much.

It was kind of like people-watching for profit.

ZIPPO LIGHTERS. BOMBER JACKETS. Furbys. Baseball cards. Beanie Babies. Levi's. Tickle Me Elmos. I got in on all of them.

Furbys were the must-have toy during the holiday season of 1998.

They were an electronic animal of indeterminate species. Were they a hamster? An owl? Whatever they were, they spoke Furbish and sold like crazy. It didn't really matter what they were or what they did—I wanted to get my hands on as many as possible. Before Christmas, I ended up with one hundred of them. I paid a lot for them—more than retail—but I sold them for a lot more. Word spread—"Hey, that pawn shop's got a bunch of Furbys"—and pretty soon there were soccer moms lined up outside the shop, pushing and shoving their way into the store like offensive linemen trying to clear out a hole.

I got Tickle Me Elmos, which I called "Epileptic Elmos." I could get away with calling them that, for obvious reasons, and we sold them as fast as they came into the store.

The perfect definition of an irrational craze, to me, is something that people can't pay enough for one year, and the next you can't give them away. The cheap-toy items on the list—Furbys, Elmos, Beanie Babies—wouldn't sell for a nickel today.

Many of the fads that earned us big money were fueled by the Japanese market. In the eighties and nineties, the Japanese market was insane. Once it latched on to something, once it decided something was the coolest thing, the people there would do anything—and pay anything—to get their hands on it. The problem, though, was timing: You had to get in early, because once they decided it wasn't cool anymore, the market fell out immediately, and with little or no warning. The arc would go straight up, then straight down.

And when *they* would go insane over something, *I* would go insane over it, too. For one thing, I went absolutely insane over Zippo lighters. In the late nineties, for reasons still not entirely clear, the Japanese decided they had to have every vintage and non-vintage Zippo lighter ever produced in the United States. I had a guy in Los Angeles tip me off about this craze.

He came into the store and asked me to cast him some little brass

Coca-Cola bottles that were flat on one side. They were about the size of a small pendant. I had two full-time jewelers working in the shop at the time, so I told the guy I'd do it for ten bucks apiece. I thought this was a little expensive, and I expected some back-and-forth, but he immediately said, "No problem."

So then I said, "I'm going to have to assess a hundred-dollar mold charge," and he said, "No problem."

I had one guy doing nothing but making these little bottles for a few weeks. We made a ton of them, and when the guy came back he said, "OK, now can you solder them onto these Zippo lighters?"

He came in with boxes of them, and we did the soldering and charged him for that. I didn't ask any questions, and one day he said, "This is the deal with the Zippo lighters, dude. The Japanese are crazy for them. I'll buy every single one of them you can find."

The more I gained this guy's confidence, the more I learned. He was buying these 1950s Zippo lighters, having us put the Coca-Cola bottles on them, and selling them for $400 or $500 apiece to another guy who knew they were fakes. In the fifties, they made these Zippos with the Coke emblem on them, and they were the most sought-after in the Japanese market. These guys were re-creating them and passing them off as authentic and selling them to the Japanese for God-knows-how-much.

When I found out I was being used as part of this scam, I refused to solder any more brass bottles onto the lighters. But I did make the first guy a deal: I'd find a way to get my hands on as many Zippo lighters as possible, and I'd sell him every single one.

I walked around swap meets handing out flyers that said, "I want your Zippo lighters. Top dollar paid." I was putting them under windshield wipers at the swap meets and grocery stores. My guy in L.A. would pay me stupid money for them, and I knew he was at least doubling and maybe tripling his money off me. I didn't give a damn. He was paying me $50 apiece for 1950s-era Zippos, and I was getting a ton of them for very little money. In one year, I made between $50,000 and $60,000 off Zippo lighters alone.

I sold some myself. The most expensive was made in the 1930s. I got $1,300 for it.

And then the market just dropped off a cliff. For no reason at all. It started for no reason and stopped for no reason.

I found out it was over when I called the guy up one day and he said, "Nope. No more Zippos. I need bomber jackets."

No problem. I made the seamless transition to bomber jackets. If you had a World War II bomber jacket, you could almost name your price. They were being sold at local swap meets and being sent to Japan. The first one I found I got $4,500 for. I got as many of those as I could, and then the fad ended as quickly as it started. That's the definition of a fad, of course. If they lasted, they wouldn't be fads. Apparently the market gets saturated, or all the cool people who are at the forefront of the trends look around and see too many people wearing bomber jackets and using Zippo lighters, so they decide it's not cool anymore and they move on to something else.

There's no rhyme or reason. There's no way to predict the product, or how much someone might be willing to pay for it. To me, it's just another example of how awesome my job is and how much fun it is to attempt to figure people out.

BASEBALL CARDS MADE ME a ton of money. Baseball cards were the hottest thing in the fad market from 1992 to 1994. Baseball cards also provide a cautionary tale.

The bible of the baseball card world is *Beckett Monthly*. It's like the Kelley Blue Book for baseball cards, and it gives prices for cards in every condition from just about every year. When baseball cards were hot, copies of *Beckett's* were lying around a lot of coffee tables.

Baseball cards were easy money for people coming into the shop looking for some quick cash. If they didn't want to bother with selling to a card shop—remember, this was before Internet commerce was a big factor—they would come into our shop and get 50 percent of *Beckett*.

It was a good deal for them—no hassle, ready cash—and a great deal for me. I would put those cards into the case and almost immediately get *more* than *Beckett*. The baseball card boom was like every other bubble in the history of economics; it typified the "irrational exuberance" Alan Greenspan attributed to the dot-com stock craze. Nobody thought baseball cards were going to go down in value, so they were willing to pay whatever it took. After all, nobody was making any more Cal Ripken Jr. rookie cards, so how could they go down in value?

I made a lot of money off baseball cards for the better part of three years. Then, in 1994, it just died. It went down in a big hurry. One reason was baseball itself; the strike/lockout hit in the middle of the 1994 season and scrapped the World Series that year. Everyone with an interest in baseball was so disgusted by that whole mess that nobody wanted to even *look* at anything related to baseball.

But the baseball card craze can teach a bigger lesson: Never collect anything that says "collectible" on it. It seems counterintuitive, but the things that end up being worth money are things nobody ever thought would be worth anything. Nobody ever thought comic books would be worth anything, and that's why you have rare comic books. Nobody ever thought pieces of cardboard with photos of baseball players would be worth anything. That's why kids put them in their bicycle spokes and moms threw them away when their sons went to college.

And that's why, for a brief period of time, they ended up being worth a lot of money. But it didn't last.

The first thing that happens when a product becomes officially "collectible" is that people leave them in the packages. They want them to be clean and pristine—they've been preached the gospel of "mint condition" forever—so they don't go down in value. Parents stop allowing their kids to put them in their spokes, and moms start thinking those packs of pristine cards will pay for college.

These "collectibles" end up everywhere. Everyone who ever watched a baseball game owned an unopened complete set of 1999 baseball cards, and they discovered they were no longer an investment. You couldn't get anything for them.

And that's how baseball cards went from being an irrational craze to being pieces of cardboard with photos of baseball players. They shot right up, they shot back down.

Collecting is nothing new. When Napoleon raided Egypt in 1798, the treasures confiscated by his army were wildly collectible. People were paying outrageous sums for anything from Egypt. The origins of collecting were a little different back then, though. If a family in the late 1700s had an item that had been signed by George Washington—or even *touched* by him—family members would pass it down through generations as a sentimental heirloom. It was collecting, but it wasn't necessarily for profit.

But when it became obvious that an item signed by George Washington could hold more than sentimental value, collecting became a capitalist enterprise. Those same family members knew it was an item of worth, and they held on to it for that reason as well. As time passed and generations became further removed, that item gradually lost its sentimental value and became primarily an object of monetary value.

At that point, it might show up in my shop.

Most irrationality is temporary. Like baseball cards, Furbys, and Beanie Babies, fads rush in and then die a quick death. But there are a million things that are permanently irrational. For instance, if you have the right Pez dispenser, it's worth thousands. Why are they different than Zippo lighters? Who knows? There are so many niche collectors and markets out there, you can make some serious observations about human nature—and make a buck or two along the way.

I spent $10,000 on what amounts to a cap-gun collection, and I got a good deal. I have a guy who knows a guy—there's a lot of that in my business—and he sent this collector to me when he found out the guy wanted to sell. He had enough vintage cap guns and Wild West toys to fill an entire room of his house. One of the sets in the collection I bought is a Bat Masterson costume made in the 1950s. It's a holster, vest, cap gun, and cane. It was featured on the show, and it's really cool. The top and bottom of the cane are actually metal. The holster is leather. You'd never find that level of detail today. It would be plastic and vinyl today.

For that one costume alone, my guy says I can get $1,000. I think I can get more.

There are so many little fanatic collectors out there. All you have to do is search message boards and fan sites on the Internet and you'll find people willing to pay money for stuff that nobody else would consider to be worth anything. That's why I laugh at some people in this country who say they're poor. I deal with people who consider themselves poor but have these elaborate collections of niche stuff. This is the only country in the world where you can be poor and have a vast collection of something.

In the 1970s, the Pet Rock craze hit. People paying money for a rock in a box because someone in a corporate office decided to call it a "pet"—this was like the ultimate practical joke on the American consumer. It was like, "Let's see how far we can take this." Well, it worked. Pet Rocks made millions of dollars. And now, if you can get an original Pet Rock, it's worth $100. I understand what you're thinking: How can you find someone to validate the authenticity of a rock? Here's the thing: It's all in the box. You have to have the right box, or else you're out of luck. The packaging is what is worth the $100, as crazy as that sounds.

Some fad products end up in my shop only *after* they run their course.

In some cases, I can make money on the back side of a fad. One example: grills. Mouth grills were made popular by rappers, and they became immensely popular in certain segments of the population. They were cool for a while, and then they weren't cool, which is when they started showing up at the pawn counter.

The first time a customer showed up wanting to pawn his grill, one of my employees came to me with a stricken look on his face.

"He wants to pawn his grill," he told me.

"OK, is it gold?"

"Yes."

"Then take it."

"But, Rick, it's still in his mouth."

"I don't care what it looks like or where it came from—it's gold. It's worth money. Pick it up with a napkin, spray it with Windex, and weigh it."

We had a lot of guys come in selling or pawning the grills right out of their mouths. They'd walk into the store and stick a hand into their mouth and pull the grill out. Some of the grills had a few hundred dollars' worth of gold in them—as much as ten or twenty grams of gold. Some had diamonds embedded in them. Damn right it was worth my time to buy them right out of someone's mouth.

I make no apologies. I have always said I would sell bat guano if there was a good enough market for it. If I knew someone who would give me more for it than I paid for it, I'd have a truck pulling up and dropping bat shit off in my driveway right now.

A DOWN ECONOMY KILLS fads. The last few years, there have been very few products that have sent consumers into a frenzy. It makes sense—when people don't have a lot of money, they're going to be more rational and less inclined to spend $200 for a $12 toy just because their kids are hounding them for it.

There are some mini-fads right now. King Baby jewelry is pretty hot. People are willing to pay a premium for anything that says "King Baby" on it. They'll pay as much as $2,000 for a bracelet.

Other than that, the biggest fad we've profited from lately is the show. *Pawn Stars* has become its own mini-craze, with our swag department selling more T-shirts and shot glasses and caps than we ever thought possible.

We have a massive rivalry within the store about who's selling the most swag—bobbleheads, T-shirts, whatever we have in the store. And you can bet we keep up with it. We check the sales figures every day for bragging rights.

The fact that Chumlee is usually the one with the bragging rights tells you something about the country, too.

I'd love to see the economy turn around so we can get back to the days of the irrational consumer crazes. I sure miss 'em.

NOT FOR SALE

**HERE ARE A HANDFUL OF ITEMS IN** the shop that we aren't interested in selling. Instead of price tags, they have tags that say "Not For Sale." For the most part, that means we've decided those items are priceless, but what it really means is I won't sell them unless the price is really, really right.

We've had people make offers on these items, but we still haven't sold them. If you put a tag on something that says "Not For Sale," it's amazing how many people decide they absolutely have to have it. There's a museum aspect to some of it; we like to keep some of our better conversation pieces around to give people a reason to come in and look around. Some of them are kept around for public relations reasons; during Super Bowl week, it's always good to let the media know we have a few Super Bowl rings in the case.

Old Man, Corey, and I make a point of saying we never fall in love with stuff we buy, but it's inevitable that some things are going to be cooler than others. We all have interests, and my interests definitely dictate the items that are considered not for sale. After all, when you've got Benny Binion's hat, you can't help but fall in love just a little bit.

THREE OLYMPIC BRONZE MEDALS

Joe Greene was a U.S. track and field athlete who won the bronze medal in the long jump in 1992 in Barcelona and 1996 in Atlanta. Both times the gold was won by Carl Lewis. Greene pawned both of his medals and never picked them up. We held them and held them, well beyond the obligatory length of time, and eventually it became clear he wasn't coming back.

Originally, I decided these two medals were not for sale because I didn't think I would ever get another one. What are the odds, right? (Plus, to have a medal from one of the American Games is beyond cool.) We've been conditioned to believe that Olympic athletes are the most committed and dedicated athletes in the world. They give up everything to train for something that—in most cases—doesn't bring a huge monetary award. For that reason, it seems unlikely that they would see the medals themselves in financial terms.

As it turned out, six months after I put the two bronze medals into the wall case behind the counter (and next to the Jim Morrison painting), I had a guy walk in with another Olympic medal.

What are the odds, right?

This guy had a medal from the 1960 Summer Games in Rome, which separates it from any other modern Olympic Games medal. The 1960 Summer Games were the only ones to engrave the sport on the back of the medal. With any other Olympiad, the medals are plain—gold, silver, bronze—with nothing to identify either the winner or the sport in which it was won.

The medal the customer was selling was a swimming bronze medal. There's still no way of telling who won it, or which event it was for, but it's pretty cool to have a medal that at least has the sport on it.

I asked the guy to tell me the story behind it, and he said, "We found it at the bottom of my grandfather's chest after he died."

"Was it his?"

"No," he said. "It's the weirdest thing: We have no idea how it got there."

Grandpa wasn't a swimmer, much less an Olympic medalist. And as far as the family knew, Grandpa didn't have a connection to anyone who was.

PATRIOTS SUPER BOWL RING

Brock Williams was a defensive back with the New England Patriots in 2001, the team's first Super Bowl–winning season. He spent most of the season, including the Super Bowl, on the injured-reserve list after blowing out his knee. A couple of years later, he showed up at the night window in the early hours of the morning with his Super Bowl ring. The night-shift guy called me at home and told me what was going on, so I came down to check it out.

The ring was legitimate, and so was he, so I wasn't concerned that it was stolen. He wanted to pawn it, not sell it, and I offered him a *lot* of money for it if he wanted to sell it. He was insistent on pawning it, and he asked for only $1,500.

A few nights later, he came back and asked if he could get some more money. Obviously, with an item this valuable, there's no problem with him getting more money. It's like a credit card, and his card was far from maxed out. But the way it works inside the shop is kind of tricky. The person adding to the loan has to first mark it in the computer as "redeemed," which usually means "picked up." And then, after that step is concluded, the employee has to start new paperwork on the new loan amount. It's just a processing thing, but it eventually becomes relevant to this story.

Williams wanted—and got—$800 more for his ring. No big deal. But when I looked at the paperwork the next morning, I saw the word "Redeemed" and the item—2001 New England Patriots Super Bowl ring—and I assumed Williams had come in and picked up the ring. Either I read through the extra $800 loan or it didn't register when I saw it.

A little backstory is in order: I have always gone through the manila envelopes containing jewelry that has come off pawn and joked, "One of these days I'm going to be going through these and the Holy Grail is going to fall out."

Old Man and I used to alternate processing the defaults every morning. He liked to open the envelopes and assess what new possessions had come our way with the changing of the calendar day. I liked it, too, and on this morning I was sifting through the envelopes when I came across one that felt different. Most of them contain jewelry—chains, rings, necklaces—but this one felt much heavier.

When I opened it up, a 2001 New England Patriots Super Bowl ring fell out.

And that is about as close to the Holy Grail as you can get.

My jaw dropped. I thought for sure he had picked it up. I walked around the office holding this huge ring, saying, "I thought for sure he had picked it up."

I set it aside for a few weeks, and still nothing. Then I decided I would display it along with my other two Super Bowl rings, one of which was the only female Super Bowl ring ever produced. (It was made for the wife of Rams general manager John Shaw.) From the beginning, I put a tag on the Patriots ring that said, "$100,000," but it's really not for sale.

This ring is a showstopper. I've gotten more publicity from having this ring than almost any other item in the shop. Whenever the Patriots made the Super Bowl in subsequent years—after the 2003, 2004, and 2007 seasons—we would put the ring on eBay with an exorbitant reserve. We had no intention of selling it, but within a day we'd receive phone calls from ten different newspapers wanting to do a story on the Super Bowl ring. And since a ton of people fly into Vegas to watch and gamble on the Super Bowl, it served to increase foot traffic as well. If a bunch of guys from Boston fly to Vegas to watch the Super Bowl, they're going to come into the shop at some point to check out the Patriots ring.

But this ring is not for sale for another reason: It's a weird ring. That's part of its appeal to me. The NFL, because it has rules for everything, has official rules regarding Super Bowl rings—size, shape, number of jewels. A team's first ring can only be a certain size, the next one can be a little bigger, and so on. I have no idea who determines the scale, but it exists.

However, when the Patriots won their first Super Bowl, their owner, Bob Kraft, said the hell with the NFL rules. He was going to do whatever he wanted with the rings. And he did. For instance, the first ring is supposed to be only ten carats, but this one's fourteen. It's only supposed to weigh so much, but this one weighs 50 percent more than the standard.

This ring is the one that broke all the rules. Now you see why I like it so much?

BENNY BINION'S HAT

Benny Binion is a Las Vegas legend. He's one of a handful of men who can legitimately say he was at the forefront of making Vegas what it is today. He was by all accounts a murderer a few times over—twice prosecuted— but he was a hell of a businessman and visionary.

He owned Binion's Horsheshoe Casino, which he immediately made famous in 1951 by making it the casino with the highest limits in Vegas. He set a craps table limit of $500, which was ten times higher than any other casino at the time. He was also the inventor of the World Series of Poker. He started out by having one-on-one poker tournaments between high rollers, and eventually he got the idea for the WSOP. Every time you see poker on television, or any time you see a local charity conducting a no-limit Texas Hold 'Em tournament, you've got Benny Binion to thank. For all his faults, he was one of a handful of people who shaped Las Vegas into what it is today.

And I have his hat. The story of how I came to have his hat is one of the more random and obscure backstories in the shop. One day an employee walked into my back office and put a Stetson 30x hat on my desk. (The designation "30x" was not a size but a percentage of beaver fur in the hat.) I looked it over—nice hat—and told him to offer $50 because I figured I could get $100 for it on eBay. I didn't give it a second thought, and I never even knew whether the employee bought it.

A month later, I was processing inventory. The guys were bringing me items, and one of them was a small suitcase. I opened it up and found it was a custom hat case with the Stetson in it. I handed it to one of the guys and told him to give it to the eBay department to sell for $100. But as I closed the lid, I noticed an old Frontier Airlines address sticker on the side. I'm always curious, so I looked at it and saw:

LESTER B. BINION
128 FREMONT ST.
LAS VEGAS, NV

Needless to say, I canceled my plans to sell the hat on eBay. A few months after the show started, Binion's daughter came in to take a look. She held it in her hands and said, "Right size, right style, right brand— that's my dad's hat."

I have to admit: I have a fondness for this hat that probably exceeds what is reasonable. I love the old Vegas characters—no matter how unsavory—and I love the story of how this hat ended up in the shop. It's the kind of classic story that typifies how cool my life is. Binion's hat occupies a prominent space in the wall case, a shelf above the Olympic medals. I've had many offers on Binion's hat, but it's not for sale. It's a piece of living Vegas history, and it's staying in the shop as long as I have a say over it.

1490 SAMURAI SWORD

First off, it was made in 1490, so that should be reason enough to keep me from selling my samurai sword. But moreover, there are practical reasons why the sword is not for sale.

This sword presents quite a conundrum. In restored condition, it's worth somewhere between fifty and sixty grand. However, there's a chip in the blade that keeps it from being in restored condition. In its current condition, I might get four or five grand for it. Big difference.

And here's the conundrum: There is one guy in the country who could fix it, and he's in Oregon. For six grand, he will re-hone the blade and fix the chip. But that process doesn't come without risk. If cracks develop in the blade during the process—a real concern in something this old—it will be ostensibly worthless.

So . . . what do you do? Risk the six grand and try to turn it into a sword worth fifty or sixty grand, knowing it might become a worthless sword? Or hold on to it and show it off as one of the coolest and oldest things in the shop?

Besides, when am I going to get another 1490 samurai sword?

TWO-HUNDRED-YEAR-OLD
JAPANESE PORN SCROLL

Maybe my worst purchase ever. I didn't really think this one all the way through. It's an amazing piece of work. It's ten feet long, with the painting on rice paper backed by silk. What is immediately striking about it is how graphic it is—phenomenally graphic for something two hundred years old. It's got several scenes, and it shows everything you could imagine in each of them. If you thought people got kinky and weird just since the Internet showed up, you ought to look at this scroll.

I tell people, "This thing would scare any young girl away from sex for life. Men simply aren't built like that."

So why is it not for sale? Simple: I can't display this thing in the shop. It would shock women (and some men) and scare kids.

Plus, my mom comes into the store. There's just no way I want her seeing this thing.

IWO JIMA BATTLE PLANS

So a guy walks into the shop and tells me his father was an army officer in the Pacific theater during World War II and he kept these battle plans in his pocket through much of the war. He unfolds them for me and they're battle plans for Iwo Jima. They're drawn in color, too.

How cool is that?

These are originals, and they're in pretty good shape. You might have seen the transaction on the show. I don't have the whole set, but I'm working on it. I have them framed and displayed toward the back of the shop, and they're some of my absolute favorite things, ever.

Knowing the importance of that battle, there's something humbling to me about looking at those battle plans and thinking about the preparation and courage it took to pull it off. And the fact that this man kept these plans throughout the war and then gave them to his son afterward is kind of awe-inspiring, too.

They ended up with me because the son needed to sell them to help finance his daughter's wedding.

He clearly didn't want to sell them, but he felt he had to. I told him, "Don't take this the wrong way, but thank God I don't have daughters."

PAWN STARS

HE RISE OF REALITY TELEVISION GOT
me thinking: What better place than here?

Nearly every day, I would sit in the shop and think
about how awesome and crazy this life is. The people,
the stories, the stuff they're selling—it's truly the most amazing job you
could ever hope to have. I would hate it, absolutely hate it, if I woke up
tomorrow morning to find that overnight everyone in the world had
been transformed into a normal, responsible citizen. That would be so
damned boring. I love the diversity we see in the shop—every race, every
religion, every socioeconomic situation, every opinion. Every day it's a
window to the world's soul.

And the night window is a window to the darkest places of the world's
soul.

So why not let everybody in on it? Why not go after a reality show
with the same resolve that marked our quest to get a full-fledged pawn
license in the first place?

After all, we were underdogs then, too.

I decided to see if I could make it happen. It became sort of an obsession with me, starting about 2005. It was rejected out of hand by a few

people, received with a pacifying nod by far more, embraced by just enough to keep me going.

By the time I set off on this wild chase, the shop was a financial success and we were pretty well set. Old Man was still micromanaging every single penny, I was having a blast learning about everything from ormolu clocks to Olympic medals, and Corey was showing himself capable of running the day-to-day operations. We were well established in Las Vegas, and all of us in the Harrison family were assured of having comfortable lives with or without television.

Tracy and I had been married for seventeen years when we had an unexpected addition to the family. Jake was born in 2003, and even though having a new baby in our late thirties—with a nineteen-year-old and a twenty-one-year-old—might not have been completely planned, it's been a great thing for all of us. He's bright and energetic and generally awesome, and he keeps us young. He and I ride bikes together and do homework together and go out into the desert and ride the quads together. I'm a big kid, so being able to act like it without having to explain myself is a great thing.

By necessity, Tracy had to work when Corey and Adam were little, but the success of the shop has allowed her to stay home with Jake. There were a lot of things that happened with Corey and Adam that I wish I could have back, and one of them is the amount of time we were around. Unfortunately, it's tough to have someone stay home when there are years you make $20,000 and have no idea if it's going to get better or worse the next year.

Tracy was happy to leave the shop behind, although she misses some of the excitement. And sometimes she misses the transvestites. But, in contrast to the way Adam and Corey were raised, we're hoping that by having Tracy stay home and raise Jake we can smooth out some of life's inevitable rough edges. I'm lucky to be in a position to do that, and we're also in a great position to help out with several charities we've adopted throughout the area.

So, you might ask, with everything running smoothly and profitably, why would I make the awkward and potentially unsuccessful move to push for a Gold & Silver Pawn Shop reality TV show?

It clearly wasn't because I thought any of us fit the role of the traditionally handsome Hollywood leading man. As you can tell, genetics in the Harrison family lean toward the overweight side of the scale, which is why I'm in the gym every morning before 6 A.M. Now, if I could force myself to eat better and cut out the damned smoking . . .

And it clearly wasn't because I wanted to show off my wardrobe. Before the show, I favored bib overalls. Hey, they're comfortable, and I really didn't care what I looked like. (Maybe it was the latent influence of Old Man's North Carolina backwoods roots.) If I had walked out of the house in matching clothes, Tracy would have had a heart attack. The concept of matching up my clothes just made no sense to me. Whenever we would get ready to go somewhere, Tracy and Corey would cringe, and Tracy would give me that "You're *not*, are you?" look. That was my cue to change.

Now I've solved the problem by always wearing Tommy Bahama T-shirts and jeans. It's foolproof—Garanimals for men.

So those are a couple of the reasons why *not*. Here are three reasons why:

First, and this should come as no surprise by now, I thought it would be profitable. Second, I thought it would be a hell of a lot of fun. Third, I thought—no, I *knew*—that it would work. Lord knows I've spent enough time in that building to understand just how unusual this life is.

Then there was another motivation: From the time I first started having seizures, I never imagined even living into adulthood. Those harrowing experiences of my childhood created a certain kind of background music in my head. If there's something I want, and I believe it's achievable, I am going to go after it with every fiber of my being.

Even though I gave up drugs and long ago stopped worrying about epilepsy, I haven't completely abandoned the recklessness of my past. I've had a total of eleven surgeries, most of them the result of dirt-bike and quad riding in the desert. One of the worst accidents came when I wrecked and tore the knob off the inside of my ankle. It slid down my foot toward my heel and sheared off several ligaments. They opened up my foot, lifted the ankle knob back into its rightful position and screwed it back in place. Another time I got twisted up on the bike and felt an ungodly amount of pain from my right foot. I looked down at my boot to see my toes pointing the wrong way.

The point is: I still do crazy stuff. To a lot of people, both inside and outside my family, chasing the dream of a Gold & Silver Pawn Shop television show was in keeping with the craziness. It didn't matter to me, though. I've tried a lot of things that have worked and a lot that failed. I wasn't afraid of failure, and I knew if I could make this a success it would be a huge success. It didn't seem like a risk at all.

I didn't know where to begin, so I did what I always do: I researched it. Acquiring an agent was the first step, and I hired an agent and tried to drum up interest from production companies. There was always interest, but I learned to decipher their language of love—everything's always great, always just about to happen—and wait for something concrete before getting too excited.

Old Man would always tell me, "Rick, you're wasting your time. You're not getting a television show."

There were times I believed him, but I also knew he wasn't looking at the world the same way I was. He'd never even watched one second of a television reality show, so he couldn't get his mind around the idea that someone might be interested in seeing how things work in a family-run

Vegas pawn shop. I had seen enough of those shows—and enough of the really bad ones—to know if it was done right, it would do well.

Tracy's response was always the same: "I'm fine with it, just so long as I don't have to be in it."

After four years of hustling around trying to make it happen, our big break came in a strange way. A television station in Los Angeles did a feature on the ten best places to shop in Las Vegas, and we made the list. I told Corey, "You watch. After this airs, we're going to get a bunch of people calling us about a TV show." Sure enough, we had fifteen or twenty calls from production companies wanting to talk about pitching a reality show to the networks.

So, after four years, we were discovered overnight.

THERE WERE TWO MAJOR players at the beginning: HBO and NBC Universal. HBO was hot to produce a pilot, so we went with them.

A year later, there was a pilot, and it didn't work for me. I have nothing against HBO. I loved *The Sopranos*, and I'm a big fan of several of their other shows, including *Boardwalk Empire*. HBO does certain types of shows really, really well. Our show, unfortunately, was not one of those shows.

HBO decided to turn it into the pawn-shop version of *Taxicab Confessions*, the show where people on a hidden camera tell their sad stories and depraved ideas to a cabdriver. Granted, there is a gritty side to our business. You could sift through the recordings from our night-window camera and get a view of the world that is quite different from the one you get on *Pawn Stars*. I don't shy away from that; it's part of life, and it's part of my business. We talk about it, laugh about it, and cringe about it in the shop. As you can tell, we aren't hesitant to admit there's a darker side to our shop and its clientele.

But the world depicted in the HBO pilot was not representative of the world I live in. They focused on the night window and treated the customers like animals in a zoo. They interviewed the customers about why they were pawning their stuff, and they would shrug and say, "This is how I get my money." It's pretty simple, but if you've never been exposed to it, it's like a foreign country.

Desperation is a part of our business, but it's a small part, and to make it the center of a reality show was misleading. It was also depressing, with no room for humor or the joy of discovery. It didn't give off the proper vibe of head-shaking wonder that takes place several times a day. Any pawn shop can lay claim to having destitute and desperate customers, but what sets us apart is the rare and unusual items and the stories behind them.

A story and a price, not a story and a vice.

The pilot never aired. We broke it off with HBO under what I would politely call "creative differences."

I still didn't give up. I knew there was a show to be made if we got the right people to share my vision. In late November of 2008, we got a call from a group called Leftfield Pictures. They called out of the blue—out of left field, I guess—to inquire about shooting a sizzle reel for a possible pilot.

It turns out some of the guys from the company had come to Vegas for a bachelor party and decided to check out the shop. It was good fortune for us, but I'd had so many high hopes and false starts that I was naturally skeptical about this one. When they said they were interested in coming out in February—three months from then—I told them there was still interest from NBC Universal.

"With the HBO thing falling through, they may want to move fast," I said before dropping every name I could remember from NBC Universal.

The lady from Leftfield said, "Let me call you back."

Fifteen minutes later she called back and said, "We'll be out there next week."

My belief in the worth of this show was so strong I had to do something to get their attention. I couldn't let it drift another few months; if they were interested now, I needed to get them into the shop *now*, before they could go off and be distracted into thinking something else was a better bet.

(Once the show started and became a hit, I told them the real story—NBC Universal was interested, but I had no idea whether a visit from them was imminent.)

Leftfield came with a crew and shot the material for a spark reel. They went back to New York and spent the next three months putting it together. Once again, this got my hopes up. These guys seemed to *get it* better than the HBO guys. They saw the enthusiasm we have for the work and the eclectic cast of characters coming through the door. This felt like it might get somewhere.

Of course, the feeling wasn't unanimous.

When I told Old Man that Leftfield was going to come in and do a sizzle reel for a show, I'll tell you what his exact words were:

"Rick, you're never going to get a fucking TV show. All this is going to be is another week of bullshit we all have to go through."

As you can tell, he's not really acting on the show. In fact, he's not acting at all. That exchange is typical of his curmudgeonly attitude. The cranky old man you see on television is the same guy I have to deal with every single day.

Anyway, they shot the sizzle reel and showed it to History on a Friday in February, and by the next Tuesday they'd ordered a pilot. It's unheard-of in the television industry for a network to move that rapidly. History had only one bit of advice: They wanted "*Antiques Roadshow* with attitude." That's a pretty good summary of what we do.

We caught it at the right time. History had hired a young woman named Nancy Dubuq to change the image of the network from "The Hitler Channel" to something more relevant and hip. She had turned around the A&E Network, and we fit into her new vision of what History could be. It could be fun and informative—classic "laugh and learn" television.

It couldn't have worked out better for us, either. In a way, the evolution of the show has followed the same path as the evolution of Gold & Silver Pawn Shop. *Pawn Stars* started out with modest aspirations—we were paid $8,000 per episode for the first season—and blossomed from there. (We're working under a much sweeter contract now.) Instead of focusing on the sordid aspects of the pawn business, Leftfield wanted to emphasize the rare and unusual items that come into the shop on a consistent basis. Through those items, they gave me and Corey and Old Man the chance to give little history lessons on the items or the events they represent—the invention of television, maybe, or the Civil War—in short cutaways. They put together a format that works, with just enough family infighting and goofy Chumlee-ness thrown into the mix.

The original name for the show was *Pawning History*. One of the guys from Leftfield came up with the ingenious idea to call it *Pawn Stars*. That was one of those why-didn't-I-think-of-it moments. Right away, we knew that was a winner.

Leftfield and History also left room for us to bring in ancillary characters like the various experts I call to give me their opinions about the veracity and worth of rare items. My buddies Tony Dee (antique firearms expert), Sean Rich (antique explosives expert), Mark Hall-Patton (the ubiquitous administrator of the Clark County Museum), and a bunch of others are regulars who add historical heft to the show. I don't *always* need them (don't tell them that), but it definitely makes for more suspenseful television when customers have to come back and get the final word on the legitimacy of their item from someone who is a known expert in the field. And there are times, I have to admit, when I've been surprised by what my experts have told me about some of the items people bring in.

One of our favorites, Rick Dale of Rick's Restorations, has been featured numerous times in the first three seasons of the show. He is our guy when it comes to cleaning up and restoring vintage items like Coke machines and a really cool antique golf cart we gave Old Man. Well, his appearances on the show prompted the first *Pawn Stars* spinoff. Rick is now the proud star of his own History show, *American Restoration*.

So *Pawn Stars* has been good for the economy. It's definitely been good for ours. As I've said, we had twelve employees before we got the television show. We now have forty-seven. When the show started, we expected an immediate spike in foot traffic. We were surprised when it didn't happen. The first few months we saw business pick up some, but nothing dramatic.

And then, as the ratings increased and the show became something of a cult hit, the spike happened. One day in December of the first television season, I looked out onto the sidewalk in front of the shop and saw more people than I could count. It hit like a storm—boom, full house.

This called for a change in how we do business. The hordes of people waiting to get into the shop forced us to hire extra security for outside, and it served to increase the exposure of Antoine the Doorman. A word about Antoine, who became yet another character from the show to get his own line of T-shirts in the swag department: He's about six-foot-six and close to four hundred pounds. If someone is getting out of line in the store, or if he suspects someone of trying to steal, he just stands up off his stool and hovers over the guy. And then as he's hovering, he puts his arms out to his sides and says, *"Really?"* It's hilarious—and effective.

We have had a line out front when we open the store at 9 A.M. every single day since then. We installed misters out on the sidewalk to keep our fans from wilting in the heat. A lot of people show up early and get confused when the front door isn't open, because the sign says "Open 24

Hours." They don't realize the night window is the only thing open from 9 P.M. to 9 A.M. And yes, people have been angry about that.

The show has created more of a draw for the odd and unusual items. I get a lot more stuff now that we're on television. People want to be on television, and we're always on the lookout for stuff that will play well on the show. Space stuff is always a hit, as well as presidential memorabilia and anything that makes you think, *I can't believe there's a market for that stuff.* Cap guns, for instance, or the guy who had an entire room of his house covered almost floor to ceiling with Transformers.

If you're out there looking at some of these collections and thinking, *No way*, I'm here to tell you there is a way. No matter how funky, there is a way.

FOR OLD MAN, THIS whole slice-of-fame thing has been both invigorating and frustrating. An old navy man through and through, he operates by the old saying "A bitching sailor is a happy sailor." The television show has completely changed his life. Instead of sitting in his chair in full view of everyone, picking through the envelopes to see what came off pawn that morning, he has to hole up in one of the cramped back offices and rely on other people to tell him what's happening out on the floor.

If he goes out, all the customers start pulling at him and asking him to pose for photographs. We have a chair set up at the far end of the showroom, near the bicycles and motorcycles, past the rows of swag, and he'll go out there a couple of times a day to pose for photographs. He's good for about twenty minutes a session before he has to come back in and smoke a cigarette.

It's a weird lark for him to have this amount of attention at this stage of his life, and we tease the hell out of him for being the favorite of all the blue-haired old gals who wander through the store and have to clutch their chests as if they're staving off a heart attack every time they see him. Still, since he's been at this the longest, the change has affected him the most.

A typical conversation with my dad since the show hit:

(Sitting in my office in the back.)
OLD MAN: *"We doing all right, son?"*
ME: *"Yeah, Dad, we're doing fucking great."*
DAD (a little sad): *"OK, son. As long as you say so."*

That's the frustrating part for him. He's been a workaholic since he was a teenager, and the biggest joys he found in the business came from work. He'd love to sit at his desk and price every item, and that's just not feasible or possible right now.

Now, with the volume we deal with, there's no way he can keep up. Everything has to be inventoried, and I tell him, "Unless you're willing to learn how to use the computer, you can't do it anymore." Well, that's a deal-breaker for him.

WE HAD ABSOLUTELY NO idea it would get this damned big. I'm on Letterman, Chum's on Leno—I mean, this is ridiculous. Look, I'm a dreamer. I had this vision of a reality show that might work for a season or two. I thought it would be fun and profitable and educational. I thought it would work, but this thing mushroomed so fast it's hard to keep up. We're on our third season, and History has already committed to a fourth.

Old Man figured he'd suffer along with my dream, but there were times when I thought he was going to refuse to be part of it. He was pretty adamant that it was never going to happen, and there was a part of me that felt the Leftfield sizzle reel was going to be our last opportunity. I'm glad it worked out, obviously, but I know deep inside I wouldn't have given up if it had fallen through.

One of the smartest things Leftfield did was choose Chumlee to be the fourth regular on the show. He's the perfect foil, and he really is that goofy—or close to it—in real life. His interactions with Old Man are classic, and the show has turned his life around more than anyone's.

I'd like to think we've helped the business emerge from the shadows a little bit, too. I think we've legitimized the pawn business by giving people an honest look at what we do. Granted, we're not the usual pawn shop, but many of the people we deal with are good, hardworking people who are forced through circumstances to live on the fringes of the traditional economy. One of the greatest validations we got was being named Pawnbrokers of the Year in 2010 for our contributions to the business.

We're building a 6,500-square-foot addition to our warehouse and office space. It's pretty crazy to think that twenty years ago we were going to court for the chance to acquire the license that would give us the right to open a pawn shop. Now one of our biggest issues is making sure there aren't too many people in the shop at any one time.

I heard a saying as a kid that resonated with me, and I've kept it in the back of my head ever since: *It's better to ask for forgiveness than permission.*

This life continues to amaze me. I'm as enthusiastic about what I do as I was the first day I started doing it. Twenty-one years of dealing with people from all walks of life has turned me into an amateur psychologist, sociologist, and anthropologist, and I still find myself reacting with amazement several times a day.

Because you know what? You never know what's going to come through that door.

ACKNOWLEDGMENTS

There are too many people to single out, so I'll keep it short. Most of the people who made this happen are the same characters who populate the book. They know who they are, and now you do, too.

Just like running a pawn shop, producing a book is a team effort. The first order of business is to thank Tim Keown. I could not have done this without him.

There are many people behind the scenes who worked hard to make this book a reality. Foremost among them is my literary agent, Richard Abate. My representatives at United Talent Agency, Feroz Taj and Ryan Hayden, deserve equal billing. They're all great deal-makers in their own right.

I'd like to thank the people at Hyperion for believing there was a book inside me. Jill Schwartzman deserves specific thanks for adopting the project and making it her own. Her expertise was both welcome and needed.